Herivelismus
— and —
The German Military Enigma

For Susan, Mary and Josie

and in loving memory of my wife

Elizabeth Maud Herivel (née Jones)

The author in 1939

Herivelismus
— and —
The German Military Enigma

Warsaw, May 1928
— to —
Bletchley Park, May 1940

John Herivel

Member of the International Academy
of the History of Science

B

M & M Baldwin

— 2008 —

ISBN: 978-0-947712-46-4

Published by
M & M Baldwin
24 High Street, Cleobury Mortimer
Kidderminster DY14 8BY, England

Printed by
Cromwell Press Ltd
Aintree Avenue
White Horse Business Park
Trowbridge BA14 0XB

Cover origination by
4Word Ltd
Unit 15, Baker's Park
Cater Road, Bristol BS13 7TT

— Contents —

Part Two: Herivelismus

Dedicated to the memory . . .

. . . of Hans Thilo Schmidt, alias Asché, whose betrayal of his fatherland and his brother, General Rudolf Schmidt, helped save the Germany of Bach, Goethe and Einstein for European civilisation,

. . . and of Gustave Bertrand of French Intelligence, who from the beginning recognised the potential importance of the Asché documents and, having seen them rejected by the French cryptographers and their British counterparts, brought them to Warsaw where they were received by the Polish Cipher Bureau as 'manna in the desert',

. . . and of the Polish cryptographers led by Marian Rejewski who with the aid of these Asché documents broke Enigma in the winter of 1932/3, producing exact replicas of its machine of which one was brought to London in August 1939,

. . . and of Dilly Knox and his colleagues in the Cottage at Bletchley Park who with the help of the British Tabulating Machine Company were responsible for using copies of this machine to prepare the sheets needed to break Enigma in France and Britain from 17/18 January 1940 onwards by means of the Polish method of Zygalski sheets,

. . . and, finally, of Gordon Welchman, who planned the building of Hut 6, and without whose immediate and unconditional support Herivelismus would have been stillborn in late February 1940, and various Military Enigma Codes—including the vital Red Luftwaffe code—would have remained unbroken beyond 1 May 1940 when the double encodement in their prefaces was dropped and the method of Zygalski sheets became inoperable.

7

— Acknowledgements —

I am indebted to the following: to the Master and Fellows of Sidney Sussex College, Cambridge, for permission to use the Mong Room for my talk on Herivelismus on 8 October 2005, and for their princely hospitality at the Master's Lodge on the night before; to Frank Carter for supplying the originals of many of the slides and to Alison Hedley for her expert preparation of them; also to Peter Lipscomb, the then Chairman of Sidney Sussex Society, for constant help between June and September 2005 without which I would have been incapable of giving a lecture in October, and later in 2007 for inestimable support in the final stages of composition. I am also indebted to Wendy Hedley for transforming the original handwritten text of my lecture into an immaculate typed version on disc, and to Kairen Bradford for effecting a similar transformation in the case of the chapters on the pre-1940 saga of German Military Enigma, for her enthusiastic assistance from 2007 onwards in the recasting of the last part of the work, and for her husband, Tony, supplying the diagrams at Appendix 1. I owe a special debt to three friends: to John Gallehawk, an archivist at Bletchley Park, for locating relevant MSS at the National Archives and sending me photocopies of many of them at a time when I was unable to visit Kew myself; to Frank Carter for re-kindling my interest in Enigma—at a time when it had begun to dwindle again after the 'Station X' programme in 1999—by mounting an exhibition of the Herivel Tip at Bletchley Park in June 2001 with the enthusiastic support of the then director Christine Large; and to Frank Carter again for access—always willingly given—to his unrivalled store of Military Enigma knowledge, especially valuable in supplementing certain parts of Welchman's epoch-making *The Hut Six Story*; to Terry Willis who gave me a signal proof of his friendship by volunteering—for I felt unable to ask him myself—to put the text and slides of the Cambridge lecture onto the hard drive of his computer, and then add to it a new handwritten appendix himself. I am grateful to my publisher Mark Baldwin for his great interest in this book and for his expert editorial advice, and also for the photographs in Figures 1, 2, 3, 4, 7 and 8 (Figs 1 and 8 by courtesy of John Alexander).

Finally, I would like to express my gratitude to all those friends and relatives—especially my daughters Susan and Mary, together with Perilla Kinchin and Margaret Willis—who helped keep my frail Enigma bark afloat after the death of my wife Elizabeth in March 2005.

— Preface —

Soon after 10 May 1940—a date which simultaneously marked the onslaught of the German Blitzkrieg in the West and the arrival of Winston Churchill at No. 10 Downing Street—another event of great importance took place in Bletchley Park when a very powerful Herivel Tip showed up for the first time in the Machine Room of Hut 6. In the preceding February I had developed the theory of Herivelismus which predicted the possible occurrence of a powerful 'cluster' on the Herivel *Square* of the day revealing the presence of a Herivel *Tip* which might then narrow down the 17,576 different values for the *ringstellung* of the Military Enigma code in question to a mere handful of possibilities. This is what now happened, and as a result the complete key on the vital Red* Luftwaffe code was determined several hours later the same day, and its messages decoded.

At a stroke, the Herivel Tip was transformed from a vague possibility to a reality, and a new method of *handbreaking* of the Red and other non-Naval Military codes was born some ten days after the method used previously had become inoperable—apart from the ephemeral Yellow code of the Norwegian campaign— following a change in German procedures on the 1 May. There were, of course, factors other than the Herivel Tip involved in the hand-breaking of all Military Enigma Codes starting with the trailblazing Red code—especially the so-called 'cillis'—but the Herivel Tip was always a

---

* The name 'Red' was given to the major Luftwaffe code by Welchman and his team prior to the foundation of Hut 6 in January 1940, though at the time they did not know how important it was going to prove. This code was said by Nigel de Grey to be 'the prime source of intelligence' for the greater part of the time from May 1940 until the German capitulation (de Grey, 'History of Sigint' p 105, para 3. NA HW3/95).

necessary factor without which no hand-breaking on a given day could ever be contemplated, as shown in detail in Chapter 12 below. It follows that without the occurrence of powerful Herivel Tips no German Military codes—apart from the Yellow code referred to above, or codes broken through the capture of monthly key books—could have been broken after 1 May for the rest of the war. This is a bold assertion, but those who find it difficult to accept need to suggest an alternative method of breaking Military Enigma beyond 1 May without the use of the Herivel Tip. Admittedly, super-computers are now able to break original German Enigma codes, but such computers were not available during the war. Nor would the Turing-Welchman Bombes—which first came on stream in late August or early September 1940—have been able to help, for they always needed cribs initially before they could function, and where could these cribs have been found in the absence of hand-breaks based on Herivel Tips? In point of fact, none of the very many non-Naval Military Enigma codes read in Hut 6 during the Second World War could ever have been put on the Bombes until they had first been provided, either directly at first hand, or indirectly at second or third hand,* with cribs collected during a period of hand-breaking based on Herivel Tips, the most striking example—apart from the Red Luftwaffe code itself—being the Afrika-Korps code or codes of 1941 onwards. Presumably it was with some of these facts in mind that my colleague of 1940 in the Machine Room David Rees—later Fellow of the Royal Society and Professor of Mathematics at Exeter University—casually remarked to me one day in the year 2000: "Of course the Herivel Tip was one of the seminal discoveries of the Second World War". At the time I was somewhat taken aback, apparently not having given very much thought to the matter myself, but I made a written note of his opinion, and on reflection I am now inclined to agree

* The meaning of 'indirectly' is explained in Chapter 12.

with him.

Some 65 years after the original discovery of February 1940, I gave a talk on Herivelismus at Sidney Sussex College, Cambridge, in October 2005. This was by far the most detailed account I had ever given. But there was one omission which was forced on me by lack of time: an almost total absence of reference to the pre-1940 historical background. For example, the fact that it would have been inconceivable for me to have imagined the idea of the Herivel Tip in February 1940 if I had not been intimately acquainted—though of course at second hand—with the German Military Enigma machine. This was through the machines used in Hut 6 which were copies of the original German machine via their replicas miraculously created by the Poles, of which two had been sent by diplomatic bag through Germany to Paris in August 1939, one for the French and one for the British, in fulfilment of a promise made by the Poles at the crucial Warsaw Conference of the preceding July.

On consideration, I was finally forced to the conclusion that the only way to fill this historical lacuna was by giving a strictly chronological, step by step, account of the whole history of German Military Enigma from its origin in 1928 to the first breakings outside Poland of the Zygalski method of sheets in France and Bletchley Park from 17/18 January 1940 onwards. The account here given in Chapters 1 to 8 covers all the essential stages of what is a seamless story, and will, I hope, resonate with my own personal account of the Herivel Tip in Chapters 9 to 12.

Part One

The German Military Enigma prior to February 1940

— Chapter 1 —

In the Beginning: The Commercial Enigma of Arthur Scherbius

Arthur Scherbius was a brilliant German engineer of an inventive turn of mind who flourished after the First World War in the leafy Berlin suburb of Wilmersdorf. There he began work on cipher machines said to have been 'large and clumsy, similar to cash registers or type-writers' and 'which operated electrically and worked on a rotor system'. We see the germ of Enigma, the name with which Scherbius ultimately christened his completed machine.[1]

From an early stage there appear to have been two distinct versions of Enigma: a light, portable model carried in a box which was supplied with a small dry battery, and a much heavier static model which ran off the mains. The portable model had a reflector in its scrambler which was missing in the large static model. The large model was on display in Berlin around 1921, so that in all probability the portable model had by then already been completed, a supposition which gains credence from the fact that Edward Travis—later to become director of Bletchley Park—recalled having bought one in 'Berlin in 1920 or 1921 or later.'[2]

By 1923 Scherbius was sufficiently confident in the future of Enigma to persuade a group of people to participate with him in the launch of a joint-stock company entitled Chiffriermaschinen Aktiengesellschaft, with its headquarters at 2 Steglitzerstrasse, Berlin. The function of the company was to make and market the invention called 'Scherbius Enigma' with Scherbius himself as managing director.[3] The flotation of the Scherbius Enigma seems to have been accompanied by a barrage of publicity in Germany and abroad; thus we hear of brochures in German and French describing the machine;[4] of Scherbius presenting his invention at a congress of the International Postal Union; of extensive coverage in Radio News; and of favourable mention from a learned Dr Siegfried Türkel in Vienna.[5] Apart from the case of Edward Travis mentioned above, distinguished cryptographers who purchased portable models of Enigma included Dilly Knox (Vienna 1925)[6] and William Friedman (U.S.A. 1929).[7]

In spite of all this publicity and apparent popularity, the company never seems to have been a great commercial success. However, in 1926 its fortunes took an unexpected turn for the better when a Captain Johannes Möller, an employee of the German Navy's cryptographic department, was ordered to proceed from Kiel to Berlin to collect a portable model of Enigma which had been bought earlier in strict secrecy from the Scherbius company. After a very careful study of the machine the Navy decided to buy a further number subject to certain modifications being made. It was this modified version of the Scherbius Enigma which was developed and used by German U-boats in the Second World War, a steckerboard having been added in 1934.[8]

Lagging some way behind the Navy as regards Enigma was the German Army, or rather the Reichswehr, for by the terms of the Treaty of Versailles the Imperial German Army had been disbanded and replaced by a full-time, 100,000-strong guard-force—the Reichswehr—intended to guarantee law and order in Germany in the face of serious disorders by Communist—and later Nazi—agitators. No doubt the Reichswehr was prohibited by the terms of the Versailles Treaty from training in Germany with heavy weapons such as tanks and long-range artillery, but such prohibitions were circumvented by the Rapallo Treaty of 1922 between Germany and Soviet Russia. For this treaty contained certain clauses which, in exchange for technical assistance to the Red Army, ensured that the Reichswehr was able both to manufacture and to exercise heavy weapons in Soviet Russia. Secret R.T. communications, however, were one topic on which no restrictions ever seem to have been placed. Here the Reichswehr had some catching up to do on the French who in the First World War had had considerable success on the Western Front in breaking R.T. transmissions of German ciphers.[9] But on 15 July 1928 the Reichswehr followed the lead of the Navy and leapfrogged over both the British and the French by commencing Enigma transmissions.[10] The French were almost certainly aware of this development,[11] but were unable to do anything about it till 1931, and the British only became interested much later in 1938; from an early stage, however, the Poles watched developments with close—and no doubt anxious—attention.

— Chapter 2 —

Mathematicians Fluent in German: The Origins of the Polish Attack on Military Enigma 1928 - 1931

After the Armistice of November 1918, Poland suddenly—and quite unexpectedly—found herself a nation again following more than a century of partition by Russia, Austria and Germany, these three powers all having been defeated in turn, the Russians by the Germans, and the Germans and the Austrians by the Allied Powers. With the break-up of the Austro-Hungarian Empire by the terms of the Versailles Treaty, Austria became an irrevocably second-rate power and posed no further threat to Poland. Not so Bolshevik Russia, and in 1919 war broke out between Polish and Bolshevik forces west of the Dnieper. This war was effectively ended by the crushing defeat of the Red Army at the Battle of Warsaw in 1920, a defeat which lifted the military menace of Bolshevism over Western Europe for a generation, and in 1921 a peace treaty was signed at Riga which guaranteed Poland's borders with Russia. This left Germany as the only one of the previous partitioning powers which still contested the boundaries of the newly freed Polish state.

After many long and difficult discussions it was finally decided at Versailles that Germany should keep East

Prussia and most of Pomerania, but that apart from the section of Pomerania ceded to Poland—including the Danzig Corridor and the status of Danzig as a Free City—decisions should be taken by plebiscites held under the auspices of the Allied Powers to decide how other regions, including Silesia and the area round Poznan, should be divided between the two countries. The eventual division inevitably left both Germany and Poland—especially Germany—deeply unhappy, and incidents short of all-out war continued down the years until the German invasion of Poland in 1939.

It is therefore not surprising to find that around 1928 the Polish authorities were paying close attention to the secret R.T. traffic of the Reichswehr—much of it inevitably passing through Polish air-space between East Prussia and the rest of the Reich—a body which could well have seemed to them the harbinger of a resurgent German Army; for the Poles—like other peoples who have suffered lengthy periods of occupation by foreign powers—would have had long memories, and been unlikely to have forgotten how Prussia had risen phoenix-like from the ashes of her crushing defeats by Napoleon at Jena and Auerstadt in 1806 in time to help turn the tide of battle at Waterloo in 1815.

The Polish interest in Reichswehr R.T. traffic intensified on 15 July 1928 when their monitoring stations reported a new type of traffic which proved 'unreadable' by members of the so-called Polish Cipher Bureau.[1] The use of the term 'unreadable' is meant here to imply that Reichswehr traffic was being read previously, but naturally this would have been cipher traffic as opposed to the new (mechanically) coded traffic after July 1928. Among the fruitless attempts to break this new traffic was possibly the employment of a recently acquired portable Scherbius Enigma to which the attention of the Poles had been drawn earlier by the famous incident of the 'misdirected crate'.[2] In late 1927 or early 1928 there arrived at the Central Post Office in Warsaw a heavy packet or crate said to contain radio equipment. A representative of the German firm concerned claimed the packet had been sent to Warsaw in error, and after strenuous efforts to have it returned to the Reich without going through Polish Customs had failed, he appealed to the German consulate to intervene. At this point the Post Office officials became suspicious and contacted intelligence at Polish G.H.Q. Two employees of the AVA Engineering Company—with whom Polish Army Intelligence had close links—were then sent over to investigate the crate; as it was now Saturday afternoon they had ample time to open it with great care, and to their surprise they found that it did not contain radio equipment. One of the two employees, Antoni Palluth, who was not only a brilliant engineer but also had a great interest in cryptology, decided that the mechanism within the packet was some sort of mechanical encoding machine. Very careful measurements and notes were then made, after which the machine was put back into its crate lacking any trace of interference, and then returned to sender on the Monday with an apology for the delay over the weekend. Alerted to the existence of such a machine, the Cipher Bureau acquired a model of the portable Scherbius Enigma which was then found to be identical to the machine examined in the General Post Office. Without the misdirected packet, the Poles would doubtless have eventually acquired a model of the Scherbius Enigma, but it might have been much later and conceivably this could have had serious consequences.

After all attempts to break the Reichswehr Enigma traffic had failed, Major Francisci Pokorny, the then director of the Polish Cipher Bureau, made an extraordinary decision: to search for mathematicians fluent in German who could do what he and his colleagues had found impossible, and break the German Military Enigma.[3] A knowledge of German might be expected to be helpful to anyone intent on breaking a German code, and in fact it turned out to be so, though it was not essential. But the need for a knowledge of mathematics was quite another matter. To see how surprising and unexpected it was one only has to contrast it with the attitude towards mathematicians in the Government Code & Cypher School (GC&CS) where they appear to have been regarded in the inter-war years as totally unsuitable members; in fact the first to be appointed, Peter Twinn, a mathematics graduate at Oxford, apparently only squeezed in because he had opted for research in Physics after graduation, a subject presumably regarded as more down-to-earth, and one which apparently absolved him from the blot of his mathematical past.[4]

Why Major Pokorny—and presumably his colleagues, including his deputy Major Guido Langer—chose mathematics as the key to unlock Military Enigma remains a matter of conjecture. Conceivably the subject had some sort of kudos among educated Poles, derived from one of their greatest national figures, Nicholas Copernicus. For although he is usually thought of—at least in Western Europe—as an astronomer, and is justly famous for his heliocentric version of the Ptolemaic system, he is known to have made only a handful of precise planetary observations, and probably regarded himself much more as a mathematician than as an astronomer, a supposition which gains credence from his famous warning to the Pope of the day: 'Mathematics is for Mathematicians'. Another conceivable source of mathematical influence could have been Austrian, since Major Francisci Pokorny was related on his father's side to Captain Herman Pokorny said to have been the outstanding Austrian cryptographer in the 1914-18 war.[5] Conceivably this Pokorny had introduced a mathematical element in his cryptography which could then have impressed his kinsman Francisci.[6]

Having set their sights on mathematicians fluent in

German, the Cipher Bureau had to decide where to find them. The answer could hardly have been in doubt: Poznan was a university town in an area which had been under German control during the whole of partition, that is, for over a century, so that the vast majority of the mathematicians among its university students could be expected to be reasonably fluent in German. Having chosen the University of Poznan as a seed-bed for their potential cryptologists, Pokorny and his colleagues took the next logical—but brilliant—step of opening a temporary branch of the Cipher Bureau in Poznan itself, where interested mathematical students could be taught the rudiments of cryptology; nothing could better illustrate their determination to leave no stone unturned to find the right mathematicians fluent in German to break Military Enigma.[7]

One of the known instructors at Poznan was Captain Maksymilian Ciężki who was the head of the German section of the Cipher Bureau but was also a trained cryptologist. In January 1939 he encountered some French and British cryptologists and lectured to them on certain aspects of Polish work on Enigma in a German said by the British to be 'only fair'.[8] But judging by his name, Ciężki must have been a Pole, so that his combination of native Polish and learnt German would have been well suited for teaching the Poznan mathematicians, and we can assume that he played the major role in the Poznan course, especially as Pokorny would have been unlikely to leave Warsaw very often, and his deputy Langer was a German-speaking Austrian with probably very shaky Polish.

The Poznan courses started in the Winter of 1928/9 and were completed by the Autumn of 1932,[9] when three Poznan mathematical graduates—chosen from among those who had attended the cryptology courses—were offered, and accepted, permanent positions in the cryptographical section of the Cipher Bureau.[10] Before that, however, in 1931, there was a development in Germany itself which was to play a profoundly important role in the successful outcome of the Polish search for Enigma, and to which we must first turn.

— Chapter 3 —

Strange Bedfellows: The Franco-German Alliance 1931–1934

We now leave the Polish Cipher Bureau to search for 'mathematicians fluent in German', and turn our attention to three persons, two German and one French, who were to make a vital contribution to the Polish breaking of Reichswehr Enigma. The first of the trio, Hans Thilo Schmidt, was born in 1888 the son of Rudolf Schmidt, director of a private educational establishment in Berlin, and his wife Joanna—whose mother was English[1]—a member of the aristocratic Prussian family von König. Hans Thilo had an elder brother Rudolf; both brothers fought in the 1914–18 war in which both were decorated with the Iron Cross for bravery; but whereas Hans Thilo ended the war as a Lieutenant, his brother Rudolf reached the rank of Captain at the H.Q. of the 4th Army. Rudolf, in fact, was a high-flyer who was retained in the post-war Reichswehr, always managed to keep close to Headquarters, and by 1936 was to be promoted to Lieutenant General.[2]

After the 1914–18 war, Hans Thilo obtained a diploma in industrial chemistry and found a position in a soap factory. He seems always to have had expensive tastes—inherited perhaps from his aristocratic mother—and he was one of those who find it easy to live beyond their means even when it lands them with mounting debts. Around 1930 he joined the army of six million unemployed in Germany, as a result of which his wife had later to go with their children to live with her parents who had returned to Bavaria, their fashionable hat shop in the Berlin Potsdammer Strasse having been closed in the great depression, doubtless for lack of wealthy clients.[3] At this point, when Hans Thilo's situation had become desperate, his brother Rudolf came to the rescue.

From 1925-1928 he had been director of the *Schiffrierstellung*, an office in the Ministry of War responsible for all army codes and ciphers later including Enigma, and when Rudolf chanced to hear that his successor, a Major Oschmann, was looking for a personal assistant, he immediately recommended his brother Hans Thilo for the position; coming from a person so influential in army circles this recommendation was as good as an order, and Hans Thilo was duly appointed. But although this position must have helped him, and he found the work in the *Schiffrierstellung* 'interesting',[4] he seems still to have been as far as ever from repaying a mountain of debts.[5] Ultimately he evidently found himself forced to think the unthinkable and find a way of releasing some of the equity tied up in the secrets of his new office, especially from Enigma, evidently the crown jewels. There must have seemed to him only one way to effect this, some foreign government would have to pay him generously in exchange for Enigma and other secrets. Having possibly first thought of the British Government, and rejected it—presumably because of the English Channel—he opted for the French. Sometime on or before 8th June 1931, with his easy, confident, aristocratic manners, he bluffed his way into the French Embassy in the Parizer Platz, and button-holed an astounded official to whom he revealed his plan for raising money from the sale of ultra-secret documents to the French Government. Eventually he obtained an address in Paris to which he wrote the following letter (translated here from the German via French).[6]

'I confirm what I said on the 8th June 1931 to your representative of the French Embassy in the Parizer Platz who gave me your address. I am in a position to bargain over some documents of the greatest importance. In order to convince you of the genuineness of my offer I have given you some references below. Your specialists will appreciate their value. Please reply before the 1st October 1931 at the following address: Hans Thilo Schmidt, 2 Kauthesgasse – Basle – Switzerland.

If there is no reply by that date I shall look elsewhere. If you give me a rendezvous, arrange for it to be on a Sunday, and preferably in Belgium or Holland close to the German border.'[7]

In a P.S. Schmidt enclosed two documents about the keys and method of utilisation of Enigma.

The Paris address given to Schmidt by the French Embassy, 75 Rue de l'Université, was the discreet premises of the so-called Deuxième Bureau housing various sections belonging to French Military Intelligence.[8] The head of section D, which concerned itself with the monitoring of foreign R.T. traffic and questions about intelligence aspects of cryptography, was a certain Captain Gustave Bertrand.[9] Ever since 1928, when French agents in Germany had reported persistent rumours that the Reichswehr had adopted a top-secret version of the Scherbius Enigma for use in their R.T. traffic—just as similar rumours had circulated earlier in 1926 regarding Naval Enigma—Bertrand had been vainly trying to discover what the actual variations were between Reichswehr and commercial Enigma.[10] His interest in arranging the interview desired by Schmidt would therefore have been intense, as was that of another member of French intelligence, a certain Rodolphe Lemoine.

Lemoine was born Rodolphe Stallman, the son of a

wealthy Berlin jeweller. He was said to have been destined to follow his father but opted instead to knock about the world for some years in Europe, Africa and South America. At some stage he married a French woman whose name 'Lemoine' he then adopted, and later her nationality by taking out French papers. In 1914 his situation would evidently have been difficult in either Germany or France, so he and his wife wisely opted to spend the war years in neutral Spain. It was there, at the age of 43, he is said to have been 'infected with a spying virus in favour of France'.* By 1931 he had become the most extraordinary figure in French intelligence circles. He lived in very great style in Paris, the source of his wealth being largely unknown though supposed to have been due in part to concessions in Africa and South America given him by the French Government in return for services rendered.[11] Lemoine was also said[12] to have been a sort of jack-of-all-trades for French Intelligence; with his help passports, false or authentic, could be obtained for any country, money or secret documents could be passed through any border no matter how well guarded, and on occasion he appears to have engaged in shady deals which threatened sometimes to embroil him with the police before French Intelligence intervened to protect him from pursuit. Gustave Bertrand, himself the soul of probity, had a very high regard for Lemoine's abilities and greatly enjoyed his company. He was, he said, "a legendary figure, of imposing status—a little too tall to pass unperceived—but whatsoever the mission entrusted to him, he always carried it off successfully." [13]

Lemoine learned of Schmidt's letter of 1st July in the middle of August and immediately went to discuss it with members of the Deuxième Bureau. Bertrand, as we have seen, was particularly impressed with its possibilities and together they went to the head of the Bureau

* Paillole, p 29.

25

and persuaded him to give Lemoine *carte blanche* in dealing with Schmidt; for Lemoine was always detailed off to be the first to meet prospective recruits to French Military—and possibly other—Intelligence Services, in order to size them up and decide if they merited a second meeting.

Before responding to Schmidt, Bertrand and Lemoine asked their man in Berlin—a certain Maurice Dejean—to check up on Schmidt. His reply came swiftly: Schmidt had indeed been received at the French Embassy on the 8th June, and he and his brother—who was a high-ranking official—both worked in the War Ministry. Also their parents, who had died recently, were well known in Berlin high society. That was enough for Lemoine who contacted Schmidt and asked him to come before noon on the morning of Sunday the 1st November 1931 to the Grand Hotel in Viviers, a Belgian town close to the border with Germany.[14]

The meeting duly took place on 1 November, and went well after a somewhat shaky start. According to Lemoine's account of 1936, Schmidt answered with increasing confidence, and in interesting detail—aided by a constant supply of liqueurs and top-quality Havana cigars—to all his questions. Later Schmidt showed Lemoine some secret documents whose authenticity was beyond question, and which convinced him that he must instantly arrange a second meeting with Schmidt to which the latter could bring as many documents as possible of the same quality, to be paid for on the spot at an agreed rate. He asked how much Schmidt earned, and when the latter replied 500 Reichsmark a month, Lemoine gave him 1500 marks to pay for his journey and the next one, after which a rendezvous was then arranged at Viviers in the same hotel for the following Sunday. For the second rendezvous, on Sunday 8th November 1931, Bertrand and Lemoine, accompanied by Bintz, the photographic expert of the Deuxième Bureau, arrived at Viviers on the Saturday.[15] Bertrand and Bintz were installed in communicating rooms of the Grand Hotel, and spent part of the night setting up photographic equipment, including lighting, in the bath of Bertrand's room, after which they tested the Leica camera to be used for photographing Schmidt's documents. The next day Bertrand awaited a call from Lemoine, installed, according to his wont, in the princely suite No. 31.[16] The call came at 10 o'clock. Bertrand describes how he went down impatient and anxious,[17] the prospects which Lemoine had opened up for Schmidt's documents being so impressive that he could only conceal his emotions with difficulty. The salon of suite No. 31 was perfumed with cigars, and there was a blare of radio—said to have been turned on by Lemoine whenever he wanted to prevent exceptionally secret conversations being overheard from outside. Lemoine presented Schmidt, who was standing with a large glass of whisky in his hand, his face illuminated by a smile. He bowed to Bertrand, clicking his heels Prussian style. He wore a cheap grey suit, and his shoes were down at heel, yet his courteous, easy manner carried an air of real distinction, and according to Bertrand his beautiful blue eyes shone with intelligence.[18]

"Monsieur Barsac," said Lemoine, using Bertrand's pseudo-name, "you are going to be very well satisfied. Monsieur Schmidt will not hesitate to give us some documents. He needs them back by 15 hours at the latest in time to catch the train to Berlin."[19] Schmidt then extracted an enormous cardboard envelope from a leather bag and handed it to Bertrand. Faced with such a large number of documents—there were a good 100 sheets some printed on both sides—which on cursory examination appeared to be of great importance, Bertrand was seized with a sort of panic.[20] Schmidt, who was himself radiant as he saw the unconcealed pleasure on Bertrand's face, gulped down a large glass of whisky and consulted Lemoine discreetly over the sum of money he might expect for the documents. Bertrand suggested 5,000 marks, but Lemoine insisted on twice that amount. "We must," he whispered "hook him defini-tively, on the spot," and Bertrand could not but agree.[21] He went up the stairs four at a time with the documents and set to work. That day Bertrand—and the photo-grapher—had no lunch! At 15 hours Bertrand descended with the manuscripts to find Lemoine imbibing cognac and smoking cigars while chatting happily with Schmidt. The joyous appearance of the two re-assured Bertrand on the outcome of their dis-cussions. As he neatly put it, "Rex's (Lemoine's code name) force of persuasion equalled his resistance to fatigue and alcohol."[22] Bertrand congratulated Schmidt, and gave him back his dossier. In halting German he asked Schmidt if he were satisfied with his conversa-tions with Lemoine, and if everything had been fixed up about future meetings. "Jawohl, meine Herren," replied Schmidt. "Alles ist in ordnung," and he bowed, clicked his heels and left the room. Bertrand was bowled over, for now he felt they held the thread which would lead to the heart of the Enigma mystery.[23]

Back in Paris, Bertrand rushed to see Colonel Laurent the head of the Deuxième Bureau who could not believe his eyes when he saw Schmidt's documents. Next day Bertrand went to see Colonel Bassières, the head of the cryptographic section at French Army Headquarters, and left him some of Schmidt's documents, emphasising their potential value for reconstituting German Enigma. But when he returned on 21 November Bassières and his colleagues gave a polite, but very firm, negative response; they simply did not, he said, have the means to use Schmidt's documents to reconstruct Enigma.[24]

In agreement with the other heads of sections at the Deuxième Bureau, Bertrand then approached 'his English friends', with two Schmidt documents. To his dismay, the response from the English cryptographers was just as negative as from the French. Bertrand was now in despair, but on the advice of his chief Colonel Laurent—who was as convinced as Bertrand of the potentially vast importance of Schmidt's documents—approached the Polish Cipher Bureau with whom a rendezvous was fixed for the 8 December 1931. At the meeting, Schmidt's documents were received 'like manna in the desert',[25] especially the two relating to the technical details and method of usage of the Enigma Machine; according to Bertrand these 'produced an explosion of stupefaction and joy.' [26]

— Chapter 4 —

The Little Room above the Saxon Square: The Polish Mastering of German Military Enigma 1933–1939

When the three 'mathematicians fluent in German' reported to the Cipher Bureau in Warsaw, they were first given a German Naval hand-cipher to work on. They were able to break this, finding their knowledge of German a considerable help.[1] But the problem of the 'unbreakable' German Military traffic remained to be solved. Instead of setting the three of them to work on this problem together, the then head of the Cipher Bureau, Colonel Guido Langer, separated Rejewski from his colleagues Zygalski and Rozycki, and gave him a small room of his own in the Polish Army HQ Building to work on Enigma.[2]

Langer was implicitly recognising that there was something special which distinguished Rejewski from his colleagues; he might have been judged the best of the three mathematicians, as he certainly was the most experienced, having spent a year's post-graduate study in Göttingen on completing his degree course at Poznan— an interesting indication of continuing academic links between Poznan and Germany post-partition; or Rejewski might have proved himself the most incisive and resourceful of the three in the cracking of the

German Naval cipher. Whatever the reason, the fact that Rejewski was set to work on the Army messages alone tells us something interesting about Langer; what we know of him makes it seem unlikely that he was a creative thinker himself, nevertheless he had evidently decided that the mastering of German Army Enigma was going to involve creative thinking of a high order, and that this could not be expected from a team of investigators breathing down each others' necks in a large well-lit room with telephones ringing and doors banging, but in a small room, by a solitary thinker, shut off from the world, and searching in the secret recesses of his mind—or of *her* mind in the case of Rejewski's illustrious compatriot Marie Curie—for the solution of some intractable-seeming problem. The youthful Newton comes to mind, unravelling the age-old problem of the origin of colours, in a small room in Woolsthorpe Manor House with nothing more than a table, two prisms, a bare wall, and the early morning sun shining through a tiny hole in the drawn curtains of his east-facing bedroom window. So I like to imagine the slightly-built Rejewski—in the uniform of a private soldier—being led along a corridor in the Polish General Staff building in the Saxon Square in Warsaw by a burly officer—either Langer or Ciężki; at some point the officer stops, unlocks a door, and ushers Rejewski into a small room with nothing but a table, a few chairs, perhaps a shelf for books, and on the table several bundles of Enigma-traffic messages and a Scherbius commercial Enigma. The officer introduces the machine and the messages, wishes Rejewski well, slams the door shut, and as his confident military footsteps echo down the corridor and gradually die away, Rejewski begins with mounting excitement to examine in detail the bundles of messages and the commercial Enigma machine, having—as we learn at Rejewski p 251—been instructed to renew the studies of Enigma abandoned by his predecessors. At this historically memorable moment the campaign for the mastery of the German Military Enigma begins in earnest.

By playing around with the Scherbius machine Rejewski would rapidly have become familiar with every detail of its structure and operation: the function of the wheels with their studs, pins, rings and serrated flanges, how they could be taken in and out of the scrambler, the function of the left-hand reflector drum, and of the right-hand in-and-out one. Above all, he would have been struck by the wonderfully ingenious way each of the three wheels was forced into the nearest of 26 equally-spaced 'allowable' positions where they were firmly held, yet not so firmly that they could not be turned by finger pressure on the flanges to any one of the 25 other allowable positions.* Also, that correspond-ing to any one of the 26 allowable positions of a given wheel there was always a different letter of the alphabet showing in the middle of the corresponding window. From this it followed that each of the $26 \times 26 \times 26 =$ 17,576 allowable positions of the three wheels in the scrambler could be fixed by a group of 3 window letters, say a b g, referring respectively to the left-hand, middle and right-hand wheels, the so-called setting of the machine. He would also quickly have recognised the 'reciprocity' of the machine, whereby if in a given con-figuration of the wheels a key-board letter, P, say, was pressed and a bulb, T, say, lit up, then if in the same configuration the key-board letter T were pressed the bulb P would be illuminated. Finally, at some stage he would have dismantled one of the wheels and discovered that the studs on one side were connected to the pins on the other by a set of 26 interior wires in an apparently random manner, and would then have probably been dismayed to calculate that there were some 4×10^{26} ways in which these connections could be made! No doubt he would have assumed that the wiring in a wheel of Military Enigma would be similar, but how could the

* See below, Chapter 10, for the above passage.

connections between its studs and pins possibly be dis-covered?

At some stage he would have turned his attention to the bundles of Enigma intercepts. It would have already been known that each intercepted message consisted of three distinct parts: a preamble in clear relating to call-signs and discriminants; after the preamble the messages consisted of 5-letter groups, but in a given message the first 6 letters were known to be quite distinct from the subsequent ones. We shall term this initial six-letter group sent in clear the *preface*, and it was to these prefaces that Rejewski must have given all his attention. It was then that he discovered a remark-able fact: if two prefaces from different messages began with the same letter, α, say, then their fourth letters would always be the same, β, say. And what was true of the first and fourth letters was also true of the second and fifth, and the third and sixth letters. From this he drew the following momentous conclusion which formed the basis of all subsequent work on Military Enigma up to 1938:

> The preface of any message of German Military Enigma was produced by the operator encoding a three-letter group α β γ of his choice twice at a certain scrambler setting. And the scrambler setting in question was the same for all messages of the day in question, but different from one day to another.

Rejewski himself, modest young man that he was, made light of his discovery, saying that it was 'readily app-arent'. Perhaps so, though it had evidently not been apparent to those members of the Cipher Bureau who had examined the Enigma traffic before him, and, as we shall see, it was certainly at the origin of his method of characteristics. Before explaining this method the following points need to be noted:

(1) The fact that the prefaces of Military Enigma contained 6 letters, effectively proved that it was a 3-wheeled machine, the wheels in question always being termed I, II and III.

(2) The fact that the scrambler setting referred to above was used by all transmitting operators on a given day, implied that it must have been part of the key of the day issued by the *Schiffrierstellung*—the Berlin office where the traitor Hans Thilo Schmidt was already the personal assistant to the director Major Oschmann.

(3) That the trio of letters α β γ was used by a transmitting operator as the message setting for encoding a given German text. And since the preface of such an encoded message was the result of encoding α β γ twice at the scrambler setting given in the key of the day, the receiving operator could decode the preface he received in clear and recover the setting α β γ (twice) with which to decode the message received.

The use of such a double encodement in the preface in a six-letter preface continued to be the Achilles' heel of German Military Enigma, both Army and later Air Force, up to 1 May 1940. The reason for using double encodement was evidently to avoid the tiresome mistakes which could arise from using a single encodement of the message setting α β γ. For, with a single encodement, the receiving operator could only test it by attempting to decode the incoming message with its use. If the German text appeared, all was well; if not, how had an error arisen in the first place? Whereas with a double encodement, if the six-letter preface led to α β γ α β γ the receiving operator would be absolutely certain that α β γ was the correct message setting. If he obtained a result such as α β γ α β δ it would be easy to track down whether the evident error was his fault or that of the transmitting operator. Nevertheless, as Rejewski commented, it might actually have been safer for the German operators to send their message settings in clear!

The fact that the first and fourth members of a six-letter preface were both produced by pressing the same—unknown—letter of the keyboard in the first and fourth positions of the scrambler, led Rejewski to the vital concept of a *cycle*. Consider the following:

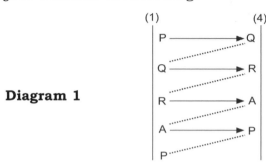

Diagram 1

Suppose P is the first letter of a preface on a given day's traffic, and Q is the fourth. This is represented in Diagram 1 by the first pair of letters P and Q at the same level immediately to the left and right of the two vertical lines (1) and (4). The arrow from P to Q is intended to indicate their connection through the unknown common keyboard letter which must have been pressed to obtain the corresponding bulb letters P and Q. Now look for the same letter Q again, but this time in the first position in another message sent on the same day. It is written directly under P and opposite, and connected to it by an arrow is the corresponding fourth letter R. Once again R is looked for among the first letters of the other prefaces, and the letter A is its companion at position 4. When this process is continued for A its position 4 companion may turn out to be P. This provides an example of a four-letter cycle: for if we proceed from a P in the first place, we shall obtain the letters Q R A P as before. Rejewski wrote such a cycle as (PQRA) where the bracket after the A implied that it would lead again to letters PQRA as before.

Such cycles could be of any length between 1 and 13, where a cycle of length 1 would arise if the first and fourth letters of the corresponding preface were identical, i.e. a 'doublet'. Rejewski gives a somewhat complicated proof that such cycles must always appear in pairs of the same length having no letters in common. This, however, can be proved directly for a cycle of any given length as follows. Consider Diagram 2:

Diagram 2

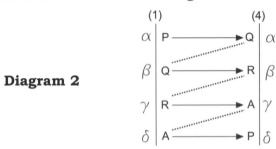

It is the same as Diagram 1 except for the new columns of Greek letters to the left and right of the lines (1) and (4). These Greek letters have the following meanings: α is the unknown key board letter which when pressed at positions 1 and 4 illuminates the bulb letters P and Q, and similarly for β, γ and δ relative to Q and R, R and A, and A and P.

We now introduce a new notation: α / P at 1, to indicate the (true) fact, that when one presses key board letter α at position 1, the bulb-letter P lights up. But from the reciprocity of the Enigma machine, if we press key board letter P at the same position 1, the bulb-board letter α will light up. So we have α / P → P / α at 1, where → is a shorthand notation for 'implies that', and we see that the 'equation' can also be written the other way round as P / α → α / P. Taking account of Q, R and A we then have the following set of implications:

I: at (1), α / P → P / α , β / Q → Q / β, γ / R → R / γ, δ / A → A / δ, and likewise.

II: at (4) α / Q → Q / α, β / R → R / β, γ / A → A / γ, δ / P → P / δ.

Armed with these results we can now construct a cycle composed of the letters α, β, γ and δ, as in Diagram 3,

Diagram 3

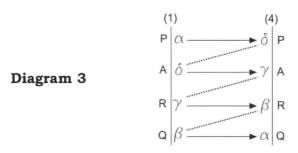

where the cycle within the (1) and (4) uprights has been bordered with certain letters from those of the original cycle (PQRA). It is easiest to pick out the items of I and II required in this bordering from Diagram 2. Thus the L.H.S. of the first row of this diagram gives α / P → P / α which is the left-hand item of the front row of Diagram 3. Also the R.H.S. of the fourth row of Diagram 2 gives δ / P = P / δ which is the R.H.S. of row 1 of Diagram 3. Therefore the whole of row 1 of Diagram 3 is correct, and the same can be easily proved for the remaining three rows. It has therefore been proved that (α β γ δ) is a cycle, as required. This proves the result for the particular case of an original cycle of four letters (PQRA), but it can be proved for a cycle of any length up to the maximum length 13.

The resulting cycle (α δ γ β) is itself quite characteristic, since starting with the sequence α β γ δ against PQRA we end up with the cycle (α δ γ β) in which the last three letters are exactly the reverse of β γ δ. It may be shown how this and similar results may be used to envisage the possibility of finding the 13 different pairs of letters resulting from pressing each of the 26 letters of the alphabet in turn at position (1). This played a vital part in Rejewski's derivation of the wiring of wheels I, II and III in the winter of 1932/3.

We cannot follow Rejewski's actual derivation of the wiring here; suffice it to say two things: (1) Starting with the notion of characteristics, he followed out a long, involved chain of arguments which jumped intuitively over many gaps and uncertainties to arrive at a set of equations involving the unknown wiring of one of the right-hand wheels of the Enigma machine used in the messages, and (2) These equations, however, involved the stecker of the code in question. Given the unimaginably large number of possible stecker pairs in any given key, Rejewski was faced with an apparently insuperable obstacle. Just about this time, however, Gustave Bertrand brought another set of Asché documents to Warsaw—in future we shall always use Hans Thilo Schmidt's code name Asché in place of his actual name—which gave the stecker for a number of recent Military Enigma codes. Knowing the stecker, Rejewski was able to solve his equations, and ultimately obtain the wiring of all three Enigma wheels. Finally, with the help of further Asché documents, he and his two colleagues were able to obtain enough information to enable the AVA Engineering Company led by Antoni Palluth to build a working replica of the Military Enigma machine.

Once the Poles had this replica Enigma, and developed methods with its help to break Enigma traffic in winter 1932/3, they continued to do so—probably almost day by day—until 1936 when the Germans began to make it more difficult by introducing an increasing number of changes to their procedures. During the period 1932–35 the wheels were only changed once a quarter; from February 1936 onwards this increased to once a month, and from October 1936 to once a day.[3] A more serious change took place in the same month when the number of pairs of stecker, previously fixed at six, began to vary between five and eight.[4] This made the so-called 'Grill' method employed by the Poles much more difficult. Later, in January 1939, the number of stecker increased to ten, where it remained thereafter. In November 1937 a new reflecting drum was introduced which was duly broken by the Poles.[5] Before that, on 15 September of the same year, a new Enigma code came on the air used by the so-called Sicherheit-Dienst of the Nazi Party;[6] this was to have very important consequences later. Finally, on 15 September 1938, the first major change in Enigma procedures took place; the method of constructing prefaces was changed radically by giving individual transmitting operators the right to choose their own indicators for each message, as opposed to the previous system in which all operators used the same indicator which only changed from day to day, and was part of the key for the day.[7] At a stroke, all the previous methods of breaking based on 'characteristics' became inoperative. New methods had to be discovered, and were discovered with extraordinary rapidity. One of these was the use of the so-called Bomba, possibly containing the germ of the Bletchley Park Bombe, and the other, discovered by Rejewski's colleague Henryk Zygalski, was the so-called method of 'sheets'.[8] This method involved punching 26 sheets for each wheel order, something which was practicable as long as there were only three wheels I, II, III with 6 different wheel orders. But on 15 December 1938 two new wheels, IV and V, were added to the original three[9] increasing the number of different wheel orders from 6 to 60, an unmanageable number for the Poles to deal with even if they knew the wiring of the two new wheels, which of course they did not. However, this piece of bad luck was balanced by an incredible stroke of good luck; the Sicherheit-Dienst, which started to use the two new wheels IV and V from 15 December 1938 onwards, only went over to the new system of indicators of 15 September 1938 on 1 July 1939.[10] The Poles therefore had a window of opportunity of some six months to find the wirings of the new wheels IV and V by employing the old method of characteristics on Sicherheit-Dienst traffic. They were triumphantly successful, their last great contribution to breaking Military Enigma. Having the wiring of all five wheels, they were thus able in principle to break Enigma by Zygalski's method. But in practice the increase in wheel orders from the six to sixty mentioned above made it beyond their physical capacity, and thereafter they could only make breaks by the method of sheets when neither of the new wheels IV and V were involved. That was the position until the all-important Tri-partite conference of Poles, British and French of July 1939. But before describing this conference, and its predecessor of January 1939, we must first look at the History of GC&CS and Military Enigma in the period 1931-1938.

— Chapter 5 —

The Years Between: GC&CS and German Military Enigma, 1931-1938

In Chapter 3, I described how Bertrand brought the first Asché documents to the Poles in 1931 after being rebuffed by both the French and British cryptographers. In 1973 Bertrand opined that the British lack of interest in the Asché documents in 1931 had been due to their unconcern at that time with what he termed the 'German menace', since in their eyes this supposed 'menace' was neither immediate nor certain, and they (the British) always needed what they called 'evidence' before they were prepared to move on any subject. 'Saint Thomas' he concluded scornfully 'would have been a worthy member of their team'.[1] Later in the same work, in a section referring to 1938, he reveals the pique he felt in 1931 at not being given a chance to argue his case with the British cryptographers whom he refers to as 'those sphinxes that nobody had a right to meet'.[2]

In an account of an interview given by Bertrand in 1936 or 1937 we get a better understanding of his motives for approaching the British in the winter of 1931.[3] It was not just that they were credited with having a powerful team of cryptographers, something they had in fact demonstrated by their decoding of the Zimmermann telegram in 1917, but that he had hoped that an encouraging British response might persuade the French cryptographers to take a more positive attitude to the Asché documents, and—although he does not actually state it—he may well have hoped that a mutually beneficial collaboration might then have been established between the French and British. From the very beginning of the Asché affair, Bertrand evidently believed—and in this was backed up by successive heads of the French Deuxième Bureau—that the Asché documents were potentially of enormous importance for breaking German Military Enigma, and since he seems to have been convinced as early as 1931 that the Germans did pose a 'military menace' to the West, he was determined to do everything in his power to bring about a collaboration between the cryptographers of those powers—including Poland, France and Britain—who had most to fear from a resurgent Reichswehr.

By 1937, the head of British Intelligence, Admiral Sinclair, alias 'Quex' or 'C' or 'Chief', had become convinced that war with Germany was inevitable,[4] a view which would have been powerfully reinforced by the Rape of Austria in March 1938, and although Sinclair and his close friend Sir Robert Vansittart the head of the Foreign Office had been 'unable to dent the shield of disbelief [in the growing military threat from Nazi Germany] that Neville Chamberlain and Lord Halifax had built to protect them',[5] as Frederick Winterbotham neatly put it, the Admiral evidently decided to go ahead regardless with contingency plans, and sometime in late 1938 or early 1939 he began to acquire a number of properties outside London to which some of the staff under his command could be evacuated in the event of war. The tenth property so to be acquired, Bletchley Park, was ear-marked for GC&CS, hence the title 'Station X' of the 1999 Channel 4 Television programme, and in this case the property may well have been acquired with the active support of Sir Robert Vansittart, the Foreign Office having been the paymaster of GC&CS civilian members since 1922.[6]

One consequence of this changed attitude to the

'German menace' would doubtless have manifested itself in an increase of interest by GC&CS in German Enigma from its very low level between 1931 and 1937. In fact, around 1937 the Chief representative of Army Intelligence at GC&CS, Colonel John Tiltman, who seems to have been seconded permanently to Bletchley Park during the war, became interested in the radio traffic between Berlin and German naval units in the Mediterranean as a result of the Spanish Civil War. This used Naval Enigma which at that time employed the same method of encodement as the Military Enigma broken by the Poles. Tiltman would have been unable to break this traffic, but he evidently got as far as characteristics, since when that system was described to British cryptographers by the Polish Captain Ciężki in January 1939, Dilly Knox found it very boring, observing to Alastair Denniston that what Ciężki described was 'what Tiltman had done'.[7] Around the same time GC&CS became interested in the commercial Enigma used by the Italians for their secret Naval communications, and Dilly Knox is said to have found the wiring of the wheels in April 1937.[8] Finally, in August 1938, following the Anschluss of the preceding March, Gustave Bertrand, who had made no attempt to interest the British in Asché since his abortive attempt of 1931, judged the time ripe for a second approach to GC&CS.[9]

This time the atmosphere was quite different, and he was able to make direct contact with Alastair Denniston and the cryptographers of GC&CS who had been converted from those 'sphinxes whom nobody had the right to meet' of 1931 into enthusiastic recipients of the Asché documents, although Bertrand, who evidently had not forgotten their earlier standoffishness, describes how he supplied the documents at first in dribs and drabs.[10] At this point Hugh Foss takes over the story: "Sometime in 1938 or 1939—Josh Cooper places the time in the Autumn of 1938 and that suits me—we were given by the Poles or the French (in fact the latter) four long steckered Enigma messages and, I believe, the stecker pairings",[11] whose working Foss and his colleagues already knew thanks to a 1931 paper from the French. The 1938 Asché documents in question would have been those described by both Rejewski and Bertrand as the plain text and encodement at given settings of a four-part practice message for German operators learning the use of the Enigma machine. The Poles, who saw several such practice messages among the documents given them by Bertrand, stated that this particular message was the only one in which the quoted key and four-part message settings actually gave on testing the quoted encoded versions,[12] and this extraordinary fact must have played a major part in the Polish breaking of Enigma in the winter of 1932/3. According to Foss,[13] Dilly Knox, Oliver Strachey, R.R. Jackson and Foss himself, all set to work on these documents from which they obviously hoped to derive the wiring of the middle and right-hand wheels of the Enigma used in the Asché document in question. For various reasons, none of these attempts succeeded. Knox with his experience of the Italian Naval Enigma would no doubt have come closest to success, but he was held up finally by his inability to guess the correct connections between the entry disc and the stecker-board. In any case, if GC&CS had been successful it would not have advanced them very far along the path the Poles—unbeknown to both Bertrand and the British—had already traversed, and which they were soon to round off by their discovery of the wiring of the two new wheels, IV and V.

Having set the British cryptographers to work on the derivation of the wiring of the middle and right-hand wheels of the machine employed by the Germans in this four-part message, Bertrand had taken the first step in a much longer-term strategy: the establishment of a full collaboration between the Polish, British and French cryptographers, especially the first two, since he makes it clear elsewhere that he had a rather low opinion of the

French cryptographers, perhaps as a result of their rebuff of the first Asché document in 1931, something he might have felt more acutely than the similar British rebuff since he had experienced the French one at first hand, and in no uncertain terms, as can be seen by the account given in Paillole.[14] It must also be emphasised that when Bertrand gave this Asché document to the British he had no inkling that it was effectively a waste of time, considering that the Poles had completely mastered Enigma; this becomes clear in a communication from Bertrand to the Poles sometime before the end of 1938 to be described below.

Immediately after describing the post-Anschluss meeting with the British, Bertrand goes on to note that he had had no new requests for documents from Colonel Langer, the director of the Polish Cipher Bureau.[15] Was it, Bertrand asked himself, because Langer knew that Asché was no longer in a position to furnish useful documents—since he had left the Schiffrierstellung in 1934—or that the Poles did not need any more help, having already all they needed to break Enigma. In any case, Bertrand decided to wait patiently. But when he had heard nothing from the Poles by December, and when as he put it, 'things looked as if they were coming to a head,'[16] —a veiled reference, perhaps, to the Munich Agreement of September 1938—he decided to write to Langer and lay before him two alternative strategies, 'one as Machiavellian as the other', an undoubted indication that he was tired of hearing nothing from the Poles on their progress, if any, in the Enigma problem and was determined to make them show their hand.

The two alternative strategies were as follows:

> *Either (1):* if it was clear that Enigma would not be broken, to let the Germans know that their traffic was being read, by supplying them through intermediaries with indubitable supporting evidence based on information received, and thus to sow

such consternation in their ranks as would force them to change their systems at a particularly difficult juncture on the eve of war. And if that strategy were agreed on, Bertrand undertook to be responsible for the deception.

Or (2): if the Poles felt that there was still some hope of breaking Enigma, to unite British and Polish 'experts' round a table in Paris where they could compare results obtained—assuming that both sides 'came clean'—when the resulting discussion might lead to progress. In the event, Langer opted for the second strategy—thus telling Bertrand that the Poles had made some progress in Enigma—provided the first was held in reserve in case the second failed. And in principle he was agreeable to a joint Polish-British meeting under the aegis of the French in Paris.[17]

Bertrand had thus taken a first tentative step towards a full Polish-British collaboration. But there were still other obstacles to be overcome; relations between the British and Polish Cipher Boards were rather cold,[18] and of course, unbeknown to Bertrand, it was to be a considerable time before relations between governments improved with the Anglo-French understanding with Poland of 31 March 1939 following Chamberlain's sudden *volte-face* after the German occupation of the whole of Czechoslovakia on March 12. Moreover, the British cryptologists—'always omniscient' according to Bertrand[19]—had to be persuaded of the need for a meeting with their Polish opposite numbers. According to Bertrand, this problem was finally solved following an interview he had with the head of British Intelligence.[20] It is possible that this meeting was with Admiral Sinclair himself, but perhaps more likely to have been with his deputy, Colonel Stewart Menzies, whom Bertrand had got to know through his own chief—Colonel Rivet—who was on friendly terms with Menzies. Assuming this to be the case, Menzies gave his permission for the suggested meeting in Paris provided Bertrand took full responsibility for the result, and Rivet in Paris took the same line.

— Chapter 6 —

Touch and Go: The Warsaw Conference July 1939

At the Paris meeting of 9 and 10 of January 1939, the Polish delegation consisted of Colonel Guido Langer, head of the Polish Cipher Bureau, and Major Maksymilian Ciężki head of the German section of the Cipher Bureau. As we have seen, Ciężki played a major role in finding the three 'mathematicians fluent in German' who were to break Enigma in the winter of 1932/3, and he seems to have done most of the talking in the third session of the conference in a German qualified by the British as 'rather uncertain.'[1] The British delegation consisted of the head of GC&CS, Commander Alastair Denniston, together with Dilly Knox and Hugh Foss. If we were to believe Bertrand's account of 1973, there was one French cryptographer present at the first session who disappeared thereafter, whereas according to Foss, whose account dates from 1949, there were several French cryptographers present who showed their methods of finding the wiring of the middle and right-hand wheels to the British delegation.[2] When they ended their exposition with a Gallic flourish *"Voilà la méthode Française"*, and asked Knox if he understood, the latter responded in such a brusque manner that Denniston and Foss had to rush in with conciliatory remarks. Ultimately, however, all was sweetness and light, and when Knox explained his method of rods the French were delighted and had made a set of *reglettes* of their own by the next séance. According to Foss the Poles were mostly silent at the first two séances whereas at the third session Ciężki gave a lengthy exposition in his uncertain German of what was evidently the method of characteristics.[3] Knox found this intolerably boring, and according to Foss kept muttering to Denniston "But this is what Tiltman did!"[4] until Denniston had to hush him down and tell him to listen politely, whereat Knox got up and stared out of the window!

The Paris meeting of January 1939 was of historic importance as the first face-to-face encounter of Polish and British cryptographers, and was to help open the way to the vastly more important meeting of July 1939, but it could hardly be called a meeting of minds, although the Poles did promise to contact the British via Paris if there was anything new to discuss.[5] The principal players, the Poles and the British, both wanted to find out what the other side knew; the Poles must soon have realised that the British knew very little, and the British were perhaps inclined to think the same of the Poles, for the copy in the National Archives of the long statement in French giving the heads of agreement for future meetings has scrawled over it 'QWE......nil'.[6] Later however, in 1948, when Denniston wrote his account of the 1939 meetings, he had come to realise that at the January meeting it was the Poles who were vetting the British rather than the other way round. In the meantime the international situation deteriorated rapidly; on 12 March 1939 the Germans occupied the whole of Czechoslovakia, and this in turn led to Chamberlain's sudden *volte-face* followed by the joint Franco-British guarantee of 31 March to Poland. War was now evidently looming, and by May the British, who had previously been rather luke-warm towards the Poles following what they regarded as 'the flop'[7] of the January conference, now became increasingly eager for news from Warsaw. When they communicated their anxiety to Bertrand he told them that the Poles were not yet ready to meet them.[8] Then suddenly in July he received a message from Langer inviting both the French and the British to a conference in Warsaw. Bertrand accepted this invitation on behalf of both countries,[9] informing Denniston on 10 July accordingly. In his message to Bertrand, Langer had spoken of 'something new',[10] an echo of the Polish promise in January to inform the French and the British if there was anything new to discuss. But the 'something new' referred to in Langer's letter probably referred not to Enigma, but to the decision taken at the highest level by the Polish Government to order their Cipher Bureau that 'in case of a threat of war the Enigma secret must be used as our Polish contribution to the common cause of defence, and divulged to our future allies'.[11] The stage was now set for the historic meeting at Warsaw from 24–26 July 1939. The French and British delegations arrived in Warsaw on Tuesday 24 July. The French delegation consisting of Bertrand and the cryptologist Braquénie—known familiarly to the British as 'Braconnier', the poacher—arrived first by air. The British delegation consisted of Denniston, Knox and Sandwith. Knox had been asked for specifically by both the Poles and the French since they knew from the January conference in Paris that he worked on Enigma. Denniston had hoped to bring other cryptologists as well as—perhaps even in place of—Knox: for he could have had a premonition in the light of the January meeting that Knox might be difficult with the Poles. If so, he was absolutely right, since, as we shall see, Knox nearly scuppered the whole conference causing extreme discomfort to Denniston on the way. Nevertheless, he was undoubtedly the right man: no-one but he in GC&CS could have grasped what the Poles had done in Enigma so rapidly and thoroughly as he did. The third man of the British delegation was Sandwith.

Sandwith was a member of Naval Intelligence, and as Denniston said of him, he was 'not a cryptologist and the Poles had no Navy'[12] but the head of British Intelligence, Admiral Sinclair, had insisted on his presence at the conference, probably on the persistent prompting of the Admiralty who as the Senior Service simply wanted to be in on the act. In fact, Sandwith's only function at the conference turned out to be as a witness of Knox's unfortunate behaviour, something which he would inevitably have reported in full to the Admiralty where it would then have passed on to Admiral Sinclair as Denniston must very well have realised. Denniston and Knox travelled by train as they wanted to see Germany for what they expected would be the last time. They would have changed trains for the Moscow express at the Templehof Station in Berlin where it is to be hoped they had time to savour some of the culinary masterpieces at the restaurant so greatly appreciated by Bertrand in his many journeys from Paris to Warsaw and back via Berlin. When Denniston and Knox arrived at Warsaw they were met at the station by the Poles and Bertrand, and possibly by Sandwith who also travelled by air. The whole party then proceeded to the Hotel Bristol—the best hotel in Warsaw—where the British delegation were to be lodged during the conference.

Later the same day, a purely formal preliminary meeting was held in a special room on the first floor of the Bristol often used for such occasions, and where the two waiters serving were specially screened by Polish security. The meeting was hosted by Colonel Stefan Mayer, head of Polish Army Intelligence—and *ipso facto* ultimately responsible for their Cipher Bureau—one of the so-called Austrian Brigade who played an important role in Polish Army Intelligence.[13] When Sandwith—the 'third man' of the British delegation—was introduced to Mayer as 'Professor Sandwith from Oxford' the latter formed the opinion that he was the most important member of the British delegation, apparently on the grounds of his extreme silence, perhaps believing that silence was an important part of what the French used to call the untranslatable *'superbe Brittanique'*. Later

51

Mayer is said to have confirmed his impression of Sandwith's importance when he confused him with General Menzies—now head of British Intelligence—whom he met in London after the war.[14]

The next day, 25 July, the Poles called for the British delegation at the Bristol at 7.00 a.m., and drove them out with the French to some 20km from Warsaw where there was 'a new strongly built and strongly guarded'[15] office in a clearing in the woods near the little village of Pyry, evidently the origin of the so-called 'Forest of Pyry' which somehow reached Bletchley Park where it passed into Enigma mythology via Welchman's *The Hut Six Story*. It was in this historic spot—whose buildings were soon to be destroyed by the Poles fleeing before the invading German forces—that the British first met the three young 'mathematicians fluent in German' including Marian Rejewski—who, as we have seen, was responsible for breaking Enigma in the winter of 1932/3—and who is commemorated today along with his two colleagues by a simple stone memorial with their names marking the spot. Alas for Denniston, and more especially for Knox, these were not the only Poles they met this day, for according to Denniston there was also one or more high ranking officers who made pompous declarations—about the Polish conquest of Enigma—which was followed by a lecture by Major Ciężki who had already bored Knox at the January meeting, and who now went on for three hours—apart from a short pause for a cup of tea—about the methods employed by the Poles for breaking Enigma. As the British expert on Enigma, Knox was closest to Ciężki and therefore in the best position to follow his discourse. Denniston, however, noticed that for some reason or other Knox reacted very oddly, and in the second part of the conference in an underground room full of electric equipment where the French and British were introduced to the Polish 'Bombas', Denniston relates how Knox continued to maintain a 'stony silence, and was obviously extremely angry about something'.[16]

One item which Denniston understandably omits at this point is made good by Bertrand who describes the astonishment of the British at seeing the Polish replicas of the German Military Enigma in the Bombas, and how they made repeated efforts to contact London to arrange for British experts to come out to Warsaw and draw up detailed plans of the replica Enigmas, only desisting when they learnt that one of these was to be sent to them via Paris on their return to London.[17]

When the various conferences in the house in the wood had ended, the British and French delegations were driven to their hotels in Warsaw. What happened then in the journey back, and afterwards at the Bristol, is best described in Denniston's own words from the account he wrote some ten years later:

> 'It was only when we got into a car to drive away [from the 'house in the wood'] that he [Knox] suddenly let himself go and assuming that no one [including the French] understood any English, raged and raved that that they [the Poles] were lying to us now as in Paris [at the first tri-partite conference of January 1939]. The whole thing was a pinch he kept on repeating. They never worked it out—they pinched it years ago and have followed developments as anyone could but they must have bought it or pinched it'.[18]

According to Denniston, on returning to the Bristol the position became 'increasingly difficult as even Bertrand, who knew no English, was aware that Knox had a grudge against the Poles who, so far as Bertrand knew, had only been successful where Knox had failed'.[19] The rest of the day remained a nightmare to Denniston: 'Knox remained aloof and alone. Bertrand, Sandwith and I discussed the situation at length and decided to get away as soon as possible'.[20]

And so, unbeknown to the Poles, matters had now reached a crisis point which constituted one of the most momentous hinges in the whole story of the mastering of the German Military Enigma. If Knox had continued to be in such a bloody-minded and intransigent mood on the morning of 27 July the conference would have been wound up, the French and British delegations would have returned home empty-handed, the further breaking of Enigma by the method of Zygalski sheets would never have taken place, and the Red Luftwaffe code would have remained unbroken, so that the Allied High Command would have been deprived of what Nigel de Grey termed 'the prime source of intelligence' for most of the time from May 1940 till the end of the war. However, by one of those strokes of good fortune which adorn the Enigma story—both Naval and Military—Knox had 'cooled down considerably'[21] the next morning from his state of incandescence of the night before, and was soon his 'old bright self'[22] again. We have no inkling of how this miraculous change took place; perhaps Bacchus, or the God of his Calvinistic forebears, had visited him with a profound slumber from which he awakened like a giant refreshed to find all his rancorous anger of the evening before had vanished away. Or perhaps he had been touched even in his anger by the modest bearing of Rejewski and his colleagues whom Denniston noted were 'all simple and straight-forward' young men 'who really knew their job.'[23] In any case, the second day—26 July—was the vital turning point of the conference during which Knox acquired an intimate first-hand knowledge of all the Polish methods of dealing with Military Enigma, especially the so-called Bomba, and the *Netz Verfahren* of Zygalski. Knox was once more 'his own bright self' and 'won the hearts and imaginations of the young men with whom he was in touch,'[24] and established a close rapport with the Poles which seems to have continued—after a pause during the German Blitzkrieg and the fall of France—at least until the end of 1940.

Knox must also have got to know Gustave Bertrand much better, Bertrand who would have watched over the cementing of relations between Knox and the Poznan three—with the French cryptologist 'Braconnier' hovering in the background—as a father watching over the reunion of his estranged children, and here it has to be remembered, and emphasised, that without Bertrand and his continuing belief in the importance of the Asché documents, there would have been no Polish miracle, no Triple Alliance, and no breaking of Military Enigma in Bletchley and Bruno by the method of Zygalski sheets between 18 January and 1 May 1940.

Before the Warsaw conference came to an end it was decided:

(1) That the Poles would send two of their replica Enigma machines through Germany by diplomatic bag to Paris, one for the French, and the other to be passed on to the British. The Poles also promised to send copies of their decodes of German Naval Enigma to London.

(2) The British, for their part, undertook to produce two complete sets of Zygalski sheets and send one of these to the Poles.

And so the Warsaw conference, from being at one point in grave danger of collapse, was saved by Knox's change of heart and turned out to be a complete success: and only just in time, for a little over a month later, on 1 September 1939, German troops invaded Poland and a few weeks later had snuffed out all armed resistance.

When news reached Polish Army headquarters in the Saxon Square that German armoured columns had broken through near Warsaw, members of the Cipher Bureau in Warsaw and Pyry were ordered to destroy or bury all sensitive material they were unable to bring with them, and make their way as best they could to

Brześć where the Polish Army planned to make a stand on the River Bug. But before they could reach Brześć, Soviet Russia entered the war on the side of Germany, and the members of the Cipher Board fled with their families to the Romanian border. There, those who were married said tearful goodbyes to their wives and children, some for the last time. They carried with them across the border two reconstructed Enigma machines, and a number of documents, in all probability including a copy of the Netz sheets for wheels I, II and III. At this point the accounts of Garlinski and Bertrand diverge. According to Garlinski the Poles were advised to go to a refugee camp,[25] but suspecting they might be interned there as a result of German pressure on Romania they pressed on with all speed to Bucharest. There they went first to the British Embassy to seek visas from their new allies. But it so happened that the Embassy was in a state of confusion following the recent arrival of the staff from the British Embassy at Warsaw, and the Poles were advised to go to the French Embassy. There they were received with open arms and were soon dispatched by train or aeroplane to Paris. In Bertrand's account the Poles stayed for a time in the refugee camp until they were located by French agents.[26] In the event, 15 Poles including the Poznan three reached Paris, and by 20 October were installed under Bertrand in the Chateau of Vignolles near the little town of Gretz-Armainvilliers which housed the headquarters of French Military Intelligence. Bertrand's party, including the Poles, were given the code name Bruno, the British representative being William Dunderdale. Up to the outbreak of the Blitzkrieg on 10 May 1940, all Franco-British communications regarding Enigma codes were sent between Bletchley Park and Bruno.

— Chapter 7 —

Honouring Promises: The Tri-Partite Alliance at Work August 1939–January 1940

When Denniston and Knox climbed into the Berlin Express and waved their goodbyes to well-wishers as the train slid past them on the platform beneath, they would have settled down into their comfortable first-class seats with very mixed feelings. On the one hand, *qua* patriotic Britons as keen as any to see Germany defeated in the approaching war, they would both have welcomed the extraordinary success of the Poles in Enigma. On the other hand, Knox would have deeply resented the role which he was cast to play in having the sheets prepared for Zygalski's *Netz Verfahren*: an important role, a vital one as it turned out, but an unfamiliar one in which the script had been written by others. Still, the fact was, the Poles had entirely forestalled him, had scooped the pool, and there was apparently no other role left for him to play in Military Enigma. As for his unfortunate outbreak on the 26th following the sessions in the station in the woods near Pyry, he would, of course, have regretted it, but—as Denniston noted some ten years later in his account of the July conference—he never referred to it again, and there was a certain patrician ruthlessness in Knox's character which would have made it relatively easy for him to push the incident out of his mind and concentrate instead on the unwelcome but necessary work which lay willy-nilly ahead of him on his return to London.

Denniston, on the other hand, who was, I suspect, of a more sensitive nature, would have found it more difficult to get over the two successive shocks he had suffered on the 25th: first, the shock of discovering that the impression he had formed at the January conference of the Poles' ignorance was false, that in reality they knew everything about Enigma, had overcome all problems, thus dashing any hopes he might have nursed that GC&CS—in the person of Knox—would have the honour and glory of unravelling the problem of the German Military Enigma. And, as if this shock were not enough, it was compounded by Knox's intolerable outbreak in the car coming back to Warsaw, and then continuing with his stony and unnerving silence in the hotel up to the point that Bertrand, Sandwith and he had decided they had no other option but to withdraw from the conference the following day.

From a letter in French written to Bertrand a few days after his return, we can see how deeply chagrined Denniston was, and how great was the pain and mortification he had suffered from Knox's behaviour.[1] It would have been easy for him to destroy the copy of a letter of such an essentially private and personal nature; that he did not do so, so that it remains today in the National Archives, can be interpreted in two ways: it may have been no more than the habit of a devoted and scrupulous civil servant; or it may have been motivated by a perfectly understandable personal desire to leave behind a record of the suffering Knox had inflicted on him in Warsaw by his wayward and unpredictable behaviour. Sandwith's presence as the third man of the delegation, foisted as we have seen on Denniston by Admiral Sinclair, probably under pressure from the Admiralty, would have been particularly galling to Denniston: he would inevitably have felt that Sandwith would retail the story of the Poles' triumph over GC&CS and Knox's unfortunate behaviour, not only to various people in the Admiralty, but also that directly or indirectly the story would find its way back to Admiral Sinclair and his deputy Colonel Menzies. Altogether, Denniston would have been justified in fearing that these revelations might damage the standing of GC&CS, and it is difficult to believe that the effective side-lining in 1940/1 of both Denniston and Knox in favour of Travis and Welchman was totally unconnected with the Polish triumph and Knox's unfortunate behaviour on the second day of the July conference. Denniston's thoughts, gloomy or otherwise, were abruptly terminated when the Berlin Express stopped at the German border. There it was discovered that through no fault of Knox his visa for the return journey was invalid. He and Denniston had then to retrace their steps back to Poznan and stay overnight while the British Consul made good the lacuna in the visa.[2] Only then could they renew their journey west, and it can be imagined with what infinite relief Denniston finally arrived back in London on the 30th July. He is said to have had an affectionate regard for Knox, but his feelings for the latter could never have been quite the same again after the tribulations of the Warsaw conference.

On the 11th of August, Denniston received a note from Bertrand informing him that he hoped to bring the 'precious object'—the replica Enigma—to London around the 16th of the month, the two replica Enigmas promised by the Poles, one for the French and the other for the British, having reached him by the first French diplomatic bag through Germany after his return from the Warsaw conference.[3] On the 16th, Bertrand duly arrived at Victoria Station[4] accompanied by Wilfred Dunderdale—the permanent representative of British Intelligence in France—carrying the precious Military Enigma machine in a sealed diplomatic bag. Awaiting them on the platform was Colonel Stewart Menzies, deputy head of British Intelligence—doubtless accompanied by Alastair Denniston—and according to Bertrand on his way to a party dressed in a dinner jacket and sporting the rosette of the *Legion d'Honneur* in his button-hole—a red-letter day in the history of Military Enigma surely deserving a blue plaque somewhere in Victoria Station. Dunderdale would then have proceeded with the 'precious object' to the offices of GC&CS where Knox would have been waiting for him, and from where it would have been sent without delay to the British Tabulating Machine Company at Letchworth. Copies would then have been produced with all possible speed and sent to Bletchley Park where they were to play a vital role in preparing the punched sheets necessary for breaking Military Enigma by Zygalski's method of sheets.

During August 1939, as war loomed ever closer, GC&CS moved from Broadway to their new war-time quarters in Bletchley Park. Things must have been very chaotic there at first, since Gordon Welchman relates how when he arrived some time later on the 4th September there was still much building of huts going on. Denniston was given a fine room in the front of the mansion, while Dilly Knox established himself and his colleagues in a small two-storied building close by called the 'Cottage'. Knox was also given a bedroom on the first floor which he used during the week, but all other members of GC&CS seem to have been allotted billets in private houses outside the Park. One of the most brilliant and colourful of these new denizens of Bletchley Park was Oliver Strachey, a member of the celebrated Strachey family, who was one of a number of senior persons billeted together in a large house in the neighbourhood. Frederick Winterbotham, senior representative of RAF Intelligence to GC&CS, and the driving force behind Hut 3 in its early days, whose contributions to Ultra seem not to have been given the attention they deserve, and who was for a while among the paying guests in this house, described Strachey as ever-smiling except when he found the owner of the house waiting at the foot of the stairs on a Saturday morning to collect the weekly rent from his guests![5]

After Britain declared war on Germany on the 3rd September 1939, new recruits began to flow into Bletchley Park. Most, if not all, of the senior civilian members among these recruits would initially have been 'spotted' by Denniston, who in late 1937 or early 1938 made a tour of British universities—with preference inevitably for Oxford and Cambridge—to find suitable candidates for the various sections of GC&CS in the event of war, including that run by Knox. Gordon Welchman relates how, having responded positively to Denniston's enquiry if he would be willing to work in GC&CS in the event of war, he was called to attend a 'course' in GC&CS in London at Broadway.[6] Having performed satisfactorily, and having, no doubt, been vetted as 'suitable' in spite of his mathematical qualifications, Welchman arrived at Bletchley Park on the 4th September, going first to Denniston who received him very warmly and told him to report to Dilly Knox in the Cottage. Apart from Knox himself, and two other members of GC&CS from London—Peter Twinn and Tony Kendrick—Alan Turing was already working with Knox in the Cottage, and John Jeffreys was to follow later. Turing, Welchman and Jeffreys were all mathematicians so that the attitude of GC&CS to mathematicians had evidently changed radically since the inter-war years when—as we have already seen—they were definitely *personae non gratae*, supposedly because of their impractical and unreliable nature.

A week or two after arriving at the Cottage, Knox asked Kendrick and Welchman to go to Elmers School nearby to study the call-signs and discriminants of Enigma traffic. Rightly or wrongly, Welchman had already gained the impression that for some reason or other Knox actively disliked him, and so he viewed this move to Elmers School as a form of expulsion, all the more so, no doubt, since before he left the Cottage he would have realised that everyone there was engaged in some form of cryptology: something he had supposed he himself had come to do at Bletchley Park, and which seemed to him not to include working with call-signs and discriminants. Later he was to change his mind, but we shall leave Kendrick and him in Elmers School thinking about what to do with call-signs and discriminants, and return to the Cottage.

Apart from Turing, who was probably giving most of his attention to developing a new sort of British Bombe based, possibly, on the Polish Bomba, and who had a room of his own on the first floor of the Cottage, the remaining members, Knox, Twinn, and later Jeffreys, appear all to have been concerned with the quickest way to produce the 1560 punched sheets needed for the functioning of the so-called Zygalski *Netz Verfahren*. This presupposed provision of an adequate number of copies of the Polish replica of Military Enigma brought to London by Bertrand and Dunderdale on the 16th August. Once available, a beginning could be made on the gigantic task of finding the position of all the 'doublets' on each of the 1560 sheets. On 1st November a memorandum signed that day by Knox, Twinn, Welchman, Turing and Jeffreys (in that order), reported that there were now sufficient Enigmas;[7] work must then have proceeded very rapidly thereafter, since from a note in French to x (Bertrand) from y (Knox) of 28 December, it appears that sheets for all 60 wheel orders were now complete, and that wheel-orders ending with a IV or a V were already on their way to Paris.[8] However, although all the punched sheets had been completed by the end of December, the British were disappointed to find that they could not use them to make a break. This seems to have led to a hold-up in sending the last lot of sheets to Paris, something bitterly resented by Knox who felt the delay was in contravention of the promise made to the Poles at the July conference. In a note to Denniston he threatened to resign if the remaining sheets were not sent to Paris 'by Wednesday night'.[9] In the event, Denniston ignored Knox's threat to resign and instead persuaded Menzies to write to Colonel Rivet—head of the Deuxième Bureau in Paris—to ask if he would allow the three Polish cryptologists to come for a short visit to Bletchley to help iron out certain difficulties [which the British were encountering in using the sheets to break Enigma].[10] However, the French could not agree to lend the three Poles—no doubt Bertrand was against it—and eventually Turing was sent over to Paris on 17 January with the remaining sheets.[11] Armed with these, the Poles began to look for the solution of what appeared to them to be a particularly favourable key, probably that of 28 October 1938, and by an extraordinary stroke of luck the first wheel order they tried proved to be the correct one. When Turing returned to Bletchley the British too were successful in breaking Military Enigma a little later, probably on or before the 27 January. According to Hinsley[12]—based on a statement in de Grey's Sigint[13]—the inability of the British to break Military Enigma prior to Turing's return from his visit of 17 January to Paris was due to faulty information supplied by the Poles regarding the turn-overs of wheels IV and V. But if this were the case, then all the 54 sets of sheets involving one or other or both of wheels IV and V would have been faulty, and only the six wheel-orders involving I, II and III could possibly work, which turned out quite definitely not to be the case. So we must look elsewhere for an explanation of the British 'problem' and I suspect it was due either to a faulty method of stacking, or may have been concerned with the method for rejecting possible solutions involving the stecker. Both of these methods would have been less familiar to Knox than to the Poles, who had broken Military Enigma by the method of Zygalski sheets for a time in 1938/9. If this was the case, Turing would have learnt of it during his visit to Paris, and would then have reported back to Bletchley Park, thus making it possible to break Military Enigma there before the end of the month.

One problem remains: how was it that all breaking of Military Enigma after the end of January 1940 took place, not in the Cottage under Dilly Knox, but in Hut 6: and what was Hut 6, and how and why was it built? To answer these questions we must return to Elmers School and its two rather lonely occupants around the middle of September 1939.

— Chapter 8 —

The Exile:
Gordon Welchman and the
Foundation of Hut 6
September 1939–January
1940

Elmers School, the place of banishment to which Kendrick and Welchman were consigned, was close to the Cottage. The discriminants and call-signs which were the object of their study were to be found in the preambles of a bundle of unbroken Military Enigma messages given them as a parting gift by Dilly. They first gave their attention to the discriminants; Welchman says that he already knew from his Cottage days that a message belonging to a particular collection of Enigma operators all having the same key on a given day, such as those concerned with Army Training, or Army Administration, or the Luftwaffe, always had one of four different three-letter groups appearing in their preamble, although the order of the letters in any particular three-letter group varied. Once the different quartets of three-letter groups could be established, then any messages having discriminants belonging to a particular quartet would be certain to have the same Enigma key on a given day.[1]

Kendrick and Welchman would not have got very far with the rather small number of messages given them by Knox. At this point the intervention of that enquiring man Colonel John Tiltman—Chief Army Intelligence representative at GC&CS—was decisive. History does not relate how he knew of the existence of Kendrick and Welchman in Elmers School; Knox may have told him of their work, or he could have learnt from them separately, or together, at the table in the dining room in the Mansion reserved for senior people in the early days of Bletchley Park. In any case, when Tiltman discovered Kendrick and Welchman were interested in discriminants he told his signals officer to give them all possible help.[2] The result was a daily flow of Military Enigma messages from the Army Interception Station perched on the top of the old fort dominating Chatham. At first Welchman did not know what to do with this flood of messages, but when he noticed Kendrick writing furiously on pieces of paper he followed suit, remembering as he did so how he had adopted the same strategy himself when he first began research at Cambridge and found himself faced with the problem of 'thinking of something to think about.'[3] Soon after this Kendrick was recalled to the Cottage, and Welchman was left to carry on working with discriminants in which he rapidly became increasingly absorbed.

Quite soon after Kendrick left, Welchman made a fundamental discovery which transformed the study of discriminants.[4] Among the many Chatham messages he noticed a number which had to be split into a group of shorter messages in conformity with the German rule that no individual message should be longer than 250 letters. But each such message had a preamble, and on comparing the resulting discriminants he was amazed to find that instead of using the same discriminant for each part—which would have given away no information whatsoever—some operators used different discriminants for the different parts. As there were essentially only four different three-letter discriminants for each key, one or two long multi-part messages were almost all that was needed to fix the discriminants for a given key.

In this way, all the different German keys coming from Chatham—and later from France—could be identified, and every day traffic could be divided into different bundles for different keys. Different keys were then given different colours, Green, Blue and Red to begin with, and the corresponding frequencies and times of the message in question plotted on large sheets of paper. This was the basis of the charts used in the Registration Room at Hut 6 from the end of January onwards. The final step, the identification of colours with different Military formations, Green with Army, Blue with Air Force Training and Red for the Main Air Force code, followed in 1940 as the number of codes broken by Zygalski's method of sheets increased from month to month. Long before that, the importance of Welchman's work on discriminants had been recognised by his being given his first assistant at Elmers School, Pat Hempsted, who looked after the colour charts and was later joined by Peggy Taylor.

Having cleared up the problem of discriminants, Welchman then turned his search-light on call-signs. Each operator belonging to any particular Enigma key or colour had a personal call-sign which varied from one operator to another. It consisted of two letters and a number, such as RA5, or any permutation thereof, all being regarded as different from the original RA5: there were therefore $(26 \times 26 \times 10) \times 6 = 40,560$ different possible call-signs. But there seemed to be no means of knowing whether an operator's personal call-sign varied from one day to the next. Here Welchman was helped by messages sent to Bletchley Park by the French which included a large number of 'Green' messages difficult to hear at Chatham.[5] Extracting all he could of this colour by means of discriminants, he discovered that many of the call-signs for a given day of the month were repeated on the same day of the preceding or succeeding month.[6] He then assumed, rightly as it turned out, that if the same operator showed up on a particular day on different months it would always be with the same call-sign. This enabled him to compile a list of some of the possible call-signs on the Green for all (up to) 31 days of the month. Armed with this brilliant result, he then asked for permission—no doubt through Tiltman—to visit the Army W.T. receiving station at Chatham. Permission having been granted, Welchman went to Chatham where he was welcomed by the director, Commander Ellingsworth.[7] They were soon on the best of terms— Welchman seems to have got on well with a certain type of bluff Naval Commander of whom Travis was an even more important example. It was from Ellingsworth that Welchman first began to get an idea of the working of nets of Enigma operators, and he also discovered the incredible ability of some of the radio operators at Chatham at picking up signals so weak as to be beyond the reach of the mechanical recording devices of the time.[8] Welchman, for his part, would have told Ellingsworth of his discovery of the monthly repetition of call-signs by a given operator, and as a result it was agreed that the preambles of all messages from Chatham would be sent in instalments by teletape to Elmers School where Pat Hempsted and her new assistant Peggy Taylor were waiting to incorporate them in the Register of the day.

Having no need to do anything more about either discriminants or call-signs, Welchman had leisure to think over something he had learnt during his short stay in the Cottage, namely the method of double encodement used by Enigma operators in the final six-letter part of their nine-letter prefaces. He probably also had some idea of the importance of doublets, and little by little he teased out a method of breaking Enigma based on collecting sufficient messages on a given day's traffic, on a particular key, whose prefaces each contained a given type of doublet. He then describes how when he finally went to the Cottage to announce this exciting discovery to Dilly Knox, he was met, not with incredulity, but with anger—this was not at all what he (Knox) had sent him (Welchman) to Elmers School to do.[9] Welchman describes his baffled surprise at Knox's reaction, but some 40 years later, when he began to conjure up memories of his early days at Bletchley Park, he thought of one possible explanation of Knox's anger: perhaps, he thought, having learnt of the Zygalski method of sheets at the July 1939 Conference in Warsaw, Knox was annoyed that Welchman had discovered something which he, Dilly Knox, had had no chance of discovering for himself.[10] Welchman's speculation on the origin of Knox's anger draws credence from Denniston's letter of 3 August in French to Bertrand;[11] for there he draws a comparison between *two* Knoxes, one the *'bon-enfant'* person—who had so charmed the three Polish crypto-graphers the day after he had been so angry with them—and the other the professional cryptographer who always wanted to be first, and could not brook compari-son with, or competition from, others. Be that as it may, Welchman relates how little upset he was by Dilly's out-break,[12] perhaps because he felt sure of himself follow-ing his unravelling of discriminants and call-signs, but also because he was delighted to find that the 'Cottage people' agreed with him that Enigma was going to be broken by the method of Zygalski sheets;[13] this set him wondering if available resources at Bletchley and Chatham would be anything like adequate for the large increase in Enigma traffic which he—rightly—foresaw in the future.

It was at this time that he began to think of Military Enigma in the widest, most general, terms. Nobody in Bletchley was more suited to do this. Thanks to Colonel Tiltman and his signals officer and his own discoveries, he knew everything there was to be known about dis-criminants and call-signs, and had incorporated this in the daily drawing up of charts which would lead to the Registration Room in Hut 6, and would stand the test of time during the rest of the war. Through Tiltman's encouragement, again, he had visited Chatham, cemented friendly relations with Ellingsworth, and had begun to learn about German Enigma nets, and the problems of capturing the traffic between their various operators. Ultimately,[14] Welchman drew up an organisational plan of which the most important factors in connection with non-Naval Military Enigma seem to have been:

A major expansion of staff—beyond the two members he had already—to a new Registration Room.

A new Intercept Room in constant touch with Chatham helping them to decide on doubtful letters in messages, if possible by checking with a second operator.

A Stacking Room with adequate staff to deal with operations on the Zygalski sheets.

Adjacent to the Stacking Room, a Machine Room where cryptographers—to whom he had already given the title of 'wizards'—would be responsible for testing the various positions thrown up by the operations in the Stacking Room.

A Decoding Room where typists provided with replica Enigma Machines would decode all the messages involved in the breaking of a given day's traffic on a particular code.

He then brought this plan to Denniston's deputy, Commander Travis, who immediately saw the urgent need for a build-up, approved the plan in full, and wasted no time in preparing for its implementation. The plan does not appear to have survived, but in its place we have the following letter to Denniston of 18 November 1939:[15]

Commander Denniston

Now that we may with some hope look forward to the state when we shall be able to deal with some of the German Enigma traffic, I think we must consider how best the traffic could be deciphered with the minimum loss of time.

If conditions remain as at present, I understand the position to be such that when the "Netz" are complete we shall be able to decipher traffic from several groups which use the Standard Indicating System. When this becomes a fact I should like to see Research divorced from Production and the work organised on the following lines:-

Research Section who should investigate the still unknown problems such as the Naval and T.G.D. This should be done by Knox, Kendrick, Turing, Miss Nugent and such of the clerks as Knox requires.

The Production Section requires dividing into several subsections as follows:-

(I) Receiving, sorting and W/T Liaison. This section would prepare data for Netz and Bombes. Staff Welshman [sic], Twinn and 4 clerks.

(II) "Netz" party. The work of finding machine settings etc., from sheets punched from cyclometer results. Jeffreys + x assistants.

(III) "Bombes" machines run by Dawson and 1 assistant

(IV) Deciphering section. This should include staff to test "Netz" and "Bombes" results. They will decipher all available traffic with minimum loss of time and pass to Service Sections for translation. It will require someone (or ones) with good German to scrutinise traffic before passing on for translation. Two female typists must be trained by R.A.F. to work their machine.

A special Hut will be required for the Production Section (Hut 6!).

18th November 1939.

We must first ask who was the author of this letter: certainly not Edward Travis who is referred to on the MS in the top right-hand corner 'Paper? by EWT'. Travis, who was at this time, and for more than a year to come, Denniston's deputy, could not possibly have written to him 'I should like to see Research divorced from Production and the work organised on the following lines...' It must then have been from someone senior to both Travis and Denniston, and that could only have been Colonel—later General—Stewart Menzies who was to succeed—or had already succeeded—Admiral Sinclair as head of British Intelligence.

There will be some supporters of Denniston and Knox who will cry 'treachery'. Not against Welchman certainly, who could not have been expected to approach Knox under whom he no longer worked, and who would naturally have approached Denniston's deputy Travis first. It is Travis' approach to Menzies over the head of Denniston which raises the question of treachery. Here we have to take account of the possibility that Travis was unable to approach Denniston first because the latter was away from Bletchley Park owing to illness. For in a memorandum of Knox dated 3 December[16] about a meeting with Denniston, the former refers to Denniston's having 'been very ill and I awaited his recovery to confess.' If Denniston had recovered by 3 December from being 'very ill', that implies that he could have been 'very ill' and away from Bletchley Park around the beginning of November, which would have given Travis just that window of opportunity he needed of seeing Menzies and persuading him of the urgency of going forward with the planning recommended by Welchman. Denniston, in fact, may have been rather glad to have been away from Bletchley when the planning decision was taken by Menzies: it saved him from the problem of selling the policy to Knox, who would, no doubt, have been unhappy at being side-lined in the Cottage while the action in Enigma was shifted to (what became Welchman's) Hut 6; in fact, Denniston later placated Dilly by telling him

> 'you could not exploit your own success and run Huts 6 and 3. I was right—you broke new ground while the building on your foundation was carried out by Travis etc, who, I say were better adapted to

this process than you. The exploitation of your results can be left to others so long as there are new fields for you to explore.' [17]

As indeed there were, especially in Abwehr.

As for Welchman, at some time between Turing's visit to Paris on 17 January, and my arrival at Hut 6 on the 29th of the month, he must have taken up his residence in Hut 6 to which all breaking of Military Enigma by the method of sheets had been transferred from the Cottage. At first there was something of a condominium between Welchman and Jeffreys who looked after the stacking room and the machine room, but Jeffreys became very ill, and at about the same time work in the stacking room was reduced after 30 April, so that Welchman must have been effectively in charge of Hut 6 from that time onwards. Long before that, sometime between November 1939 and March 1940, he had made an extremely important contribution to the breaking of both Military and Naval Enigma by the invention of the so-called Diagonal Board, which when incorporated into the Turing Bombe revolutionised its performance from September 1940 onwards.[18]

— *Part Two* —
Herivelismus

— Chapter 9 —

Setting the Scene: Belfast, Cambridge, and Bletchley Park

In 1929 I failed an examination for scholarships open to all pupils of my year at the Methodist College, Belfast. Some time later, however, I was asked to see the Head of the Maths Department—a brilliant teacher called Thomas Fazackerly—who told me I had done a very good paper in mathematics and invited me to come into his class the following term. Summer past, I returned to school where I first checked up my mathematics class. To my dismay I found I was not on the list for the top class, that I still languished in the third. I was bitterly disappointed. I had set my heart on Fazackerly's class, and he had simply forgotten his invitation. I found I couldn't accept that and decided I must find a way to remind him. A day or two later I shot out of the third class after the bell, and ran to Fazackerly's class near by. The door was still closed and I took up my station and waited. Soon the door burst open and pupils poured out, but not Fazackerly who was talking to someone inside. As I heard him moving towards the door I steeled myself. When he finally appeared, some internal force or other impelled me forward to bar his way. "Sir," I cried, "you told me I would be in your class this term, and I'm not." Instead of flying into a rage at my impudence, he cast up his eyes in the curious way he had of remembering things, as I learnt later. "You're right, come tomorrow, then," he said, after a pause, and he moved on as I stepped aside.

In *The Hut Six Story* Welchman asks what would have happened if I had not come to Bletchley Park. But he was not to know that I would infallibly *not* have come if fate or destiny, call it what you will, had not impelled me forward willy-nilly to take that tide once missed which never comes a second time: for that *was* the tide in the affairs of this boy that I was, mathematically speaking, and therefore Enigma-wise. For to make a very grand comparison, just as the inscription over the entrance to Plato's Academy in Athens warned that nobody could enter there who did not understand mathematics, so nobody was recruited to the Machine Room in Hut 6 who was not a mathematician; mathematicians, moreover, who were of two sorts only: those who had been students of Welchman's at Sidney Sussex College, and those who had been friends of his at Cambridge; in other words, he had packed the house!

I never thought very much again about the Fazackerly incident—although I never forgot it—until 2004, when I asked myself how exactly it was I came to Bletchley Park in January 1940, and then realised for the first time how determinative it was.

Once in Fazackerly's class I rose easily to the top and stayed there for the rest of my time at school, choosing mathematics as my principal subject in Sixth Scholarship, and later going up to read it at Cambridge in 1937, at Sidney Sussex College, with Welchman as my supervisor. Malcolm Chamberlain—who also came to Bletchley—and I were supervised by Welchman for a total of six terms in all, during which we concentrated almost entirely on problem-solving—for we got the theory from lectures—Welchman setting us two or three problems each week—the mathematician's essay—whose solution or otherwise he discussed the next week, and so on.

When I returned to Cambridge in the Michaelmas term of 1939, I was found fit for military service but was told to go on with Part III of the Mathematics Tripos in the meantime, having obtained a First in Part II as an accelerated student at the end of two years, in no small measure due to Welchman's supervision in problem-solving as already noted. The war was already more than a month old, and in the East, Poland had been wiped off the map of Europe for the second time after 21 years of freedom following more than a century of partition. But in that brief period the cryptographers of the Polish Cipher Bureau had comprehensively broken the German Military Enigma, something totally unknown at the time outside Poland.* However, in 1939, after the British and French Governments had given solemn undertakings to come to Poland's aid if attacked by Germany, the Polish Government instructed their Cipher Bureau to hand over all their secrets in Enigma to the French and the British, something which finally took place—in the very shadow of war—between 24 and 26 July 1939†—facts unknown to all but a handful of persons in Britain not including Welchman.

Welchman had already disappeared from Cambridge by the time I arrived there; rumour had it that he was doing war work of great importance—but of an unspecified nature—in Bletchley. One evening early in the second term I was in my rooms in college when there was a knock at the door, and in came Welchman himself. After a few civilities—he was evidently pushed for time—he told me that he was doing very important war work at Bletchley, and would I like to come there and

* See Chapters 2 and 4 above.　　† See Chapter 6 above.

help him? It did not take me very long to make up my mind; the university was a ghostly place, Part III of the Mathematics Tripos could wait till after the war, and I agreed to come. He then told me where to go, on which day, whom to ask for, and after bidding me "*Au revoir*", vanished as swiftly as he had come.

A few days later I found myself rattling along the Bletchley line, wondering what fate held in store for me; I was to find out surprisingly soon! I arrived at Bletchley Park on 29 January 1940, a date I remember as the same day of the month as my birthday. Having signed, or possibly sworn, the Official Secrets Act under the unfriendly eye of a Commander Bradshaw, mitigated somewhat by the presence of his charming secretary, I was told where my billet was, and directed to Hut 6 where Malcolm Chamberlain and I were soon being taught about Enigma by Alan Turing and Tony Kendrick. Turing—that extraordinary man—was much more interested in the wiring of the wheels and the permutations involved in finding them than in the machine itself, and a great deal of what he said must have gone straight over our heads. But Kendrick was more down-to-earth, and quite soon Malcolm and I had a firm grasp of the working of Enigma, and were passed down the line to David Rees who had come to Bletchley Park at the end of December, and who enlightened us on the so-called 'method of sheets' for breaking Enigma codes. This method had been successfully used by the Poles for a short time in pre-war Poland, but it was only very recently—on the 17/18 January—that it had worked for the first time outside Poland. That was in France, at Bruno, where the Polish cryptographers had found asylum after fleeing Poland soon after the outbreak of the Second World War. A few days after 18 January, a second code was broken for the first time by the same method in Bletchley Park itself, not in Hut 6—which was still not completed at that time—but in the Cottage under Dilly Knox.

At this time in early February there was no shift working, so I returned each evening to my billet close by in one of a long line of terraced houses in the road sloping down from the level of the Park towards the railway bridge. I had been given a sitting room in the front part of the house, and when the landlady—alias the lady of the house who had been required by an all-powerful war-time government to give *me* board and lodging in *her* house—had cleared away the supper dishes, said "Good Night"—I hope I stood up as she did so—and closed the door, I was then totally cut off from the outside world except for the occasional faint Proustian sound, through the tightly drawn curtains, of the shuffling feet of some lost soul toiling up or down the hill in the deep snow outside—for the winter of 1940 was an exceptionally severe one. As for me, each evening I was soon installed in a very comfortable late Victorian or early Edwardian armchair before the fire, always hissing and spitting as it got really under way, backed up by a full scuttle of coal, enough to see me halfway through the night.

When I look back on this simple scene, so indelibly etched on my memory in which nothing else about the house or its inhabitants—not even my bedroom— remains, I realise how providential it was that I was the unique billettee: otherwise, I would never have got within a mile of Herivelismus, for happy tranquillity and Wordsworth's 'bliss of solitude' were the *sine qua non* of what I was unwittingly about.

A few weeks on in February was a very lean time indeed for the Polish method of sheets, and it would not have been surprising if people other than myself had been casting around for a new way of breaking Military Enigma. Be that as it may, I distinctly remember doing so every night in front of the fire for a week or so from around mid-February onwards, always concentrating on the encoded messages, and always totally without any glimmer of progress. Then suddenly one night something very strange happened; I may have dozed off before the fire—a dangerous thing to do as I often smoked a pipe and might have burnt a hole in my landlady's carpet or worse—and perhaps I woke up with a start and the faint trace of a vanishing dream in my head. Whatever it was, I was left with a distinct picture—imagined of course—in my mind's eye, of a *German Enigma operator.*

This was the trigger that was to set off my discoveries, though of course I had no idea of it at the time. But I may have felt I was close to something, and that I would have to be very careful not to miss it, like the proverbial ships passing in the night. So I seem to have taken Aristotle's advice, that you cannot really understand anything thoroughly unless you see it growing from the beginning. In this case, the beginning would be early in the morning when the wretched operator would have to wake or be wakened and *set up the new key of the day on his machine.* To understand how this was done, however, will need some knowledge of the German Military Enigma to which we now turn.

— Chapter 10 —

The German Military Enigma Machine: Its Structure and Working

All Enigma machines (see Figure 1) contained four distinct parts: a stecker-board (**SB**), a key-board (**K**), a bulb-board (**B**) and a scrambler (**Sc**). We shall concentrate first on the scrambler, seen in Figure 2 with a drum on the left-hand side, followed by three wheels each with a letter tract and a serrated disc (Fig. 10 below), and a second drum on the right-hand side.

Figure 1: 3-wheel Enigma (inner cover open at right)

Figure 2: The scrambler of the 3-wheel Enigma

Figure 3: Enigma wheels

As regards the wheels, see first Figure 3. At the left, there is the left side of a Military Enigma wheel with 26 studs equally placed around a circle, and at the right the other side with 26 pins equally round a circle. In all Enigma wheels the studs and the pins were connected together by internal wires which allowed current to flow

81

from one side to the other. By 1940 Military Enigma had five different wheels from which a selection of three was chosen every day according to the operators' key book; these three could be chosen in sixty different ways. The chosen three were then threaded on an axle which was placed in the scrambler lying horizontally on two supports, one on each side. In Figure 4 the axle has been withdrawn from the machine with two wheels still on it and the other slid clear with some of the 26 equally spaced letters of the 'letter tract' or 'ring' of the wheel clearly visible.

Figure 4: Enigma wheels and axle

We now turn to the *ringstellung* of the wheel shown at the right of Figure 4, the account to be given being a simplified version of a reality which could only be seen on an actual machine. What I shall call the *ringstellung* button can be seen with a small mark on it opposite the letter V of the ring: imagine oneself, then, holding the wheel in one's left hand, and attempting to push the button along the ring in either direction with the right hand: it will not budge. But if the small stud near the button is moved sideways, the button may be pulled clear of the ring which can then be spun round freely in either direction relative to the body of the wheel: what had seemed at first to be an immovable part of the wheel is now found to be capable of independent motion. As for the button, instead of slipping through one's fingers into the well between the letters and the serrated disc (Fig. 5) and onto the floor, it turns out to be attached at one end to a spring whose other end is screwed into the side of the well further down. If one brings the ring round until some other letter, say A, is roughly opposite the button, the rounded end of the latter will soon encounter a cavity exactly opposite A into which it fits closely, and where it is then held by the pressure of the spring: we then say that the *ringstellung* (i.e., in English, the ring setting) of the wheel has been changed from its original value V, to a new value A.

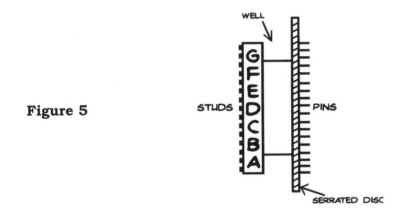

Figure 5

Now that the notion of *ringstellung* has been introduced, we are in a position to understand the term 'key of the day'. Each branch of the German Military had its own particular Enigma code which was indicated in Hut 6 by a particular colour; for example, there was a Luftwaffe code which was given the colour Red by the Hut 6 Registration Room, and there were two different Army codes, one for training and one for administration, which were given the colours Blue and Green respectively. Each operator belonging to a given German code had a monthly key-book containing changing values for wheels, *ringstellung* and stecker for each day of the month. We are not concerned with the stecker beyond noting that although the Germans must have thought they made Military Enigma totally unbreakable, in reality they presented no real problem to Hut 6: if we were going to break Enigma for a particular day, either by the Polish method of sheets, or by hand, we always found a discrete number of possibilities for wheels and *ringstellung* first; and having found these, there were various possibilities for the stecker which were systematically ruled out through internal contradictions, leaving one possibility for which no contradictions could be found and which then gave the correct solution.

A typical entry in an operator's keybook for a given day for wheels and *ringstellung* might be

III I V   D H P

where the Roman numerals referred to the wheels, and the letters to the corresponding *ringstellung*. The operator would then lift the previous day's wheels out of the scrambler, set the left-hand wheel III at *ringstellung* D, the middle wheel I at H, and the right-hand wheel V at P. He would then thread the wheels back onto the axle in the correct order with pins to the right and studs to the left, and return the wheels on the axle back in the scrambler. The wheels were then 'loose' as in Figure 6.

LOOSE

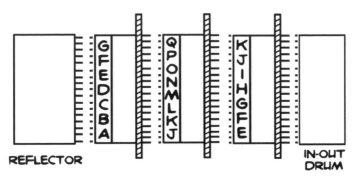

Figure 6: Enigma wheels before clamping

REFLECTOR

IN-OUT DRUM

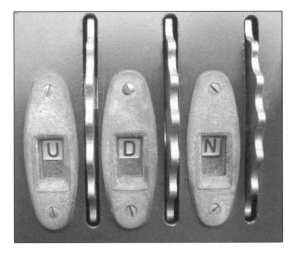

Figure 7: Wheel letters seen through windows

Finally, before encoding a message, the operator had first to turn on the so-called compression bar, and then bring down the inner lid to a horizontal position. The effect of turning on the compression bar was twofold: first, the left hand drum moved to the right and compressed the wheels together so that they no longer had any play between them to left or right: second, each wheel was forced to move up to ½ Scherbius—where 1 Scherbius, named after the inventor of the Enigma machine = 360°/26 = 13.846°—clockwise or anti-clockwise so that when the inner lid was brought down into a horizontal position *there was always a letter in the middle of each window* (Fig.7); at the same time, each serrated disc had been so positioned that it passed through the opposing slit and projected above the level of the lid (Fig. 8). Each wheel was now held 'tight' (Fig. 9) by one of three brushes* attached to the compression bar which had reached its closest position to the axle by pressing in firmly against a trough of the serrated disc opposite it. By applying pressure by hand on the ser-rated disc (Fig. 10) of the wheel in question the latter could be pushed or pulled one Scherbius either clock-wise or anti-clockwise until it reached a new position of 'rest' at one or other of the nearest troughs; a new letter immediately before or immediately after the previous one would then be found in the window. In this way each of the letters in the windows could be given any desired value; and in all the 17,576 possible rotor positions every stud had a pin exactly opposite it, and *vice versa*, so that perfect electrical contact was always maintained.

* a convenient name for rotating rubber wheels

Figure 8: The serrated discs projecting above the lid

TIGHT

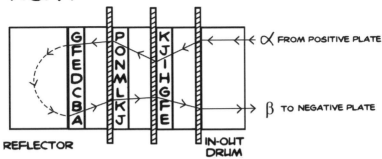

Figure 9: Enigma wheels clamped together

Figure 10

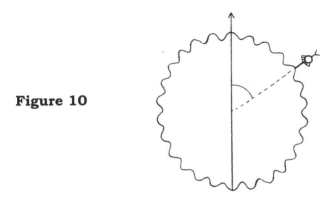

In this diagram a serrated disc is represented for simplicity of understanding by a sinusoidal curve down which the brushes of the compression bar can slide into their final positions, rotating the disk clockwise or anti-clockwise as a consequence. The cylindrical compression bar carries three brushes of which one is ultimately forced tightly by the bar against the nearest trough of each corresponding serrated disc. In reaching their final positions of rest as near as possible to the axle of the scrambler, the serrated discs, and the wheels of which they form part, are forced to rotate up to ½ Scherbius clockwise or anti-clockwise. In the diagram the brush appears set to make contact with one of the *crests* of the serrated disc in question. If this were actually to occur the bar would be jammed against the serrated disc in question before the brush reached its position of closest contact with the wheels. In reality any of the brushes would always first make contact with one side or other of a crest, and the consequent rotation of the disc referred to above—and with it the wheel—would ensue.

Finally, the positions of the disc troughs relative to the *ringstellung* buttons must have been arranged in each wheel at the time of construction so that when the wheel is held firmly by the opposing brush one of its letters is *exactly* in its pole-position. This will ensure that when the internal lid is rotated down to a horizontal position *there will be a single letter squarely in the middle of each of the windows*. Although the pressure of the brushes is sufficient to hold the wheels firmly in these positions, it is not so great as to prevent any wheel being pushed or pulled by hand pressure on the projecting part of a disc (see Fig. 8) to another position where it can again be firmly held by the brush with a new letter in the window, for the rotation of the disc (and with it the wheel) between two successive trough positions is always one Scherbius and therefore the second position is bound also to have a letter exactly in the middle of the window.

The operator was now ready to encode a message. First he thought of a three-letter setting for the scrambler, say HIT. He moved the left-hand wheel round till H was in the window, and similarly for I and T in the middle and right-hand wheels. He then pressed the first letter of the message, say 'α'. The right-hand wheel moved anti-clockwise through 1 Scherbius until U was in the window, and then stopped: if the letter α was held down, current would then pass from the positive plate of the battery, eventually reaching the negative plate via the bulb-board where the filament of the bulb through which the current passed lit up the letter β, say, above it. As long as the key α of the keyboard was held down β would be lit. Curiosity at this point prompts one to ask the following question: supposing the operator turned back the right-hand wheel from U to T, and pressed the letter β, which bulb would light up? Inevitably, and correctly, the answer would be α. These results are expressed in Figure 11 where the asterisk indicates a *bulb letter*. This is an example of the *Reciprocity of the*

Enigma, something which can easily be proved from the wiring diagram of the machine. Without it the machine would have been useless, and if Scherbius had been unable to arrange for it he would have thrown Enigma aside.

RECIPROCITY
If $a{\rightarrow}q$ * at HIT,
then $q \rightarrow a$ * at HIT.

Figure 11

Now let us see how a message was encoded and decoded. Having set his machine at HIT, the operator typed out the message, the result being given to the right of the arrow in small Greek letters (Fig. 12), the asterisks indicating that they were bulb letters, taken down on his pad by the operator's assistant. The encoded message was then transmitted by R.T. to the receiving operator who, by a method to be explained later, discovered the correct message setting HIT. On typing out α β   .... (on the left at the line below) a sequence of bulb letters ensued which was taken down by his assistant and consisted of the German text of the original message: for if S gave α* at HIT, as it did, then by reciprocity α must give S* at HIT, which was the first letter of the German text, and so on for all the other letters.

AT HIT   STRENG (GEHEIM...) EN → αβ𝛾𝛿ε𝜍(......) η𝜚

Figure 12   AT HIT   αβ𝛾𝛿ε𝜍(......) η𝜚 → STRENG (GEHEIM...) EN

THE ASTERISKS INDICATE THEY ARE "BULB LETTERS"

— Chapter 11 —

Illuminations:
The *Ringstellung* Insight
and its Development

When I interrupted my story to explain about Enigma, including setting up the key for the day, my imaginary German operator was just about to do so himself. It was at this point of my solitary musings before the fire that I suddenly had a thought. In imagining him setting up the key, I had supposed that he would have changed the *ringstellung* in each of the wheels before threading them on the axle. But supposing he had not? Supposing he had changed the *ringstellung* *after* the wheels had been put in the scrambler and were still 'loose'? What then? It was at this point I had my first illumination; I saw in a flash that such an operator, provided he did not disturb the wheels too much after setting their *ringstellung* before going off to sleep again, *might possibly leave the* ringstellung *of the day in the neighbourhood of the pole-positions: Lemma I.* Why? Before answering this question we must do some imagining. Imagine threading three wheels on their axle. Then place the axle in the scrambler where it sits horizontally on two supports, one at each end. The wheels are now vertical. They are also loose. Imagine one of them spun round: every particle of it will describe a vertical circle with centre somewhere on the (imaginary) central line of the axle, and so will the *ringstellung* 'button' as illustrated in Figure 13. The centre of the circle is on the axial line and we imagine looking at it from a point along the axle on the right hand side of the machine. As the wheel as a whole spins clockwise (seen from the right-hand side) the button will move clockwise round the perimeter of the circle. The line through the centre is supposed vertical, a horizontal line through the centre would divide the circle into two semi-circles of which the lower one represents the 'well' of the scrambler, a cavity in which the lower halves of the wheels sit, not to be confused with the 'well' of an Enigma wheel in Figure 5: if the button is anywhere there it will be invisible—remember there are really three wheels, and drums at each end. Finally, the pole-position already referred to is the highest point of the circle above its centre, just above 0 where the central line cuts the circumference. The darkened area extending 2½ Scherbius on each side of the pole will be termed the *neighbourhood* of the pole.

Figure 13

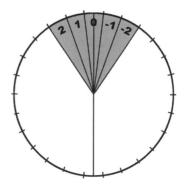

Now we return to the question *why*. For the following reasons: if you have to change the *ringstellung* of a wheel held 'loosely'—you obviously cannot do it if it is held 'tightly' by the compression bar—you will need to get a finger on the *ringstellung* button first, and for that it must not be out of sight in the well under the axle, or too low on one side, or too far over on the other: in fact the change can be effected most easily if the wheel—not the ring—is spun round—button and all—until the button is somewhere in the neighbourhood of the pole-position, the point where you can lean over it and move it most easily once freed by the nearby stud.

This immediately leads to the Lemma I: because if the button is in the neighbourhood of the pole-position—as it is assumed to be—then when the letter opposite the button, namely the *ringstellung* letter of that wheel for the previous day, is changed to the new *ringstellung* letter of the day—by temporarily withdrawing the button and spinning round the ring before replacing the button—the new *ringstellung* letter will, like the button which is opposite it, also be in the neighbourhood of the pole-position. Hence the original Lemma I: Q.E.D.

When the operator had set the *ringstellung* buttons for all 3 wheels in the neighbourhoods of the pole-positions, there were certain other things he had to do before going off to sleep again if he were not to leave himself in serious dereliction of duty; first he had to turn on the compression bar, then he had to lower the inner lid into a horizontal position, move the stecker-board lid into a vertical position, and finally close, and probably lock, the large outer lid. His machine would then be portable, ready for a quick get-away if necessary, and safe from marauding ants and other troublesome insects which could easily interfere with a free flow of current later on. Notice the order of the first two acts was a forced one: because the inner lid cannot be lowered into a horizontal position before the compression bar has been turned on, since it is this act which, among other things, moves the three wheels to the right into exactly the positions where each serrated disc fits into its respective slit.

Once the compression bar had been turned on, and the inner lid made horizontal, there would *be a letter exactly in each window.* For this to be the case, each wheel would have to have been moved by means of its serrated disc—as explained on page 85 above—up to half a Scherbius* clockwise or anti-clockwise, the exact number of degrees, and the sense of the rotation, being

* see above, p85

completely independent from one wheel to the next. Each of the *ringstellung* buttons would have participated in the rotation of its wheel. If the rotation were clockwise, the button in question would move closer to the pole-position; if anti-clockwise, it would move farther away; but in any case one would not have had to take too large a grain of salt to assume all the buttons remained more or less in the neighbourhoods of their respective pole-positions.

Now suppose that, in one of the wheels, some letter α was the one in the window, it is proved in Appendix I that the hole opposite α would be in its pole-position. We then have:

(i(the pole-position is opposite the letter α in the window, and
[ii] the *ringstellung* button is opposite the *ringstellung* letter

But from Lemma I we assume that the *ringstellung* button is in the neighbourhood of the pole-position. Therefore from 2. the *ringstellung* letter will be in the neighbourhood of the pole-position, and therefore from 1, the *ringstellung* letter will be in the neighbourhood of the letter in the window α, which implies that the letter in the window α will be in the neighbourhood of the *ringstellung* letter.

We can now enunciate the following *modified* Lemma I:

An operator who changes his *ringstellung* when the wheels are already in the scrambler, having set his new key of the day around 1 am, *may* go off to sleep again leaving his machine locked up for the night *with the letters in the windows in the neighbourhood of the* ringstellung *of the day*. I shall call such an operator a *rogue operator*, not because he set his *ringstellung after* he put the wheels in the machine, but because he then failed to twiddle them backwards or forwards well away from their positions near the poles.

Let us now see how this modified Lemma might help break Military Enigma. For this we have to return to the process of encoding and decoding which assumed the receiving operator had some way of knowing the true message setting used by the transmitting operator. For that the latter had to construct a 'preface' which can be explained in conjunction with Figure 14.

HITHIT AT LER
$$\longrightarrow \alpha\beta\delta\partial\epsilon\varsigma$$

Figure 14

$$\alpha\beta\delta\partial\epsilon\varsigma \text{ AT LER}$$
$$\longrightarrow \text{HITHIT}$$

LER is a new three-letter setting, chosen by the transmitting operator and called the *indicator*, at which he encodes the message setting HIT twice, resulting in six bulb letters represented by the six small Greek letters α β γ δ ϵ ζ. LER followed by the six—after 1 May 1940 to be replaced by *three*—small Greek letters made up the *preface*. This preface was then sent *in clear* before the encoded message. The receiving operator being in the loop would immediately set his machine at LER and encode α β γ δ ϵ ζ, when—as can easily be seen by reciprocity—he would obtain HITHIT. *Wunderbar!* He was now quite certain that the true message setting was HIT which, of course, was the reason for the double encodement—a fatal error, as it happened, since it enabled the Poles and the British to break Military Enigma by the method of sheets up to 30 April 1940. After this date there was only one encodement, but the method was the same.

94

The receiving operator then set his machine at HIT and by reciprocity obtained back the original German text as explained in the preceding chapter. Armed with this notion of *indicator* we can now understand my second illumination; imagine a rogue operator, who in accordance with the modified Lemma, happens to have left his window letters locked up in the neighbourhood of the *ringstellung* of the day. Suppose he is wakened out of his sleep again early in the morning with a most urgent message to encode for transmission. He is *very* sleepy, and/or possibly frightened by a loud explosion or other incident of war, and finds it difficult to think of anything at all, let alone the necessary three letters of his indicator, whereupon he simply takes the letters he finds waiting siren-like in the windows of his machine for his first indicator of the day. It follows that this indicator, which is sent in clear as part of the preface and may be in the neighbourhood of the *ringstellung* of the day, will then be intercepted by our station at Chatham and sent to Hut 6.

Hence the original expression of Herivelismus:

> Examine together (in a way to be explained) all early indicators of the day on a given code, and if there is a *cluster* (to be explained) among them it may give some idea of the *ringstellung* of the day.

Enunciated sometime in the second half of February 1940, this theorem was proved to be true following the first hand-break of the Red (Luftwaffe) code soon after the following 10 May. However, a closer examination of the theorem than I was able to give in the Cambridge reconstruction of October 2005 has convinced me of the inadequacy of Lemma I and modified Lemma I on which it is based. This inadequacy is due to the following facts:

> The angular positions of both the *ringstellung* letters and buttons relative to their respective pole-

positions are undefined.
The notion of 'oppositeness' between corresponding letters and buttons is imprecise.

Both these lacunae are removed in Appendix I where the
result referred to in the proof of the modified Lemma I is
justified.

I have no recollection of it, but I feel sure I would have
gone early the next day to check up at least the first version of Lemma I on my machine. Welchman—who was
often away on business—was very fortunately present,
and unhesitatingly clutched at this interesting straw,
encouraging me to follow it up, and—what was much
more important—showed his confidence in the possibilities of this curious theory of his ex-student by immediately getting his friend Commander Ellingsworth at
Chatham to send up prefaces early to Hut 6. Evidently
we were looking for quick solutions! Little did we know!

I must now explain the *examining together of indicators*
and the notion of *clusters,* in the so-called Herivel
Square. This can be seen in Figure 15, which is taken
from Welchman's *The Hut Six Story.* There are thirty
indicators below the square. Let us first see how they
were all put on the square. Take *HDR.* Go along the
horizontal axis to *H.* Then go up vertically until you are
opposite the second letter *D* on the vertical axis, and in
the resulting small square write the third letter *R,* the
convention being that H, D and R refer to the left-hand,
middle and right-hand wheels. All the other indicators
were treated in the same way. If you look at the resulting entries on the square you will see that there is a distinct cluster in the top left-hand corner surrounded by a
black line bounded by the T/U horizontal line above, the
Q/R horizontal line below, and the E/F and H/I vertical
lines to the left and right (taken from the top horizontal
axis). Finally, the letters in this 3x3 box are between I, J
and K apart from Q which we reject as a dud.

96

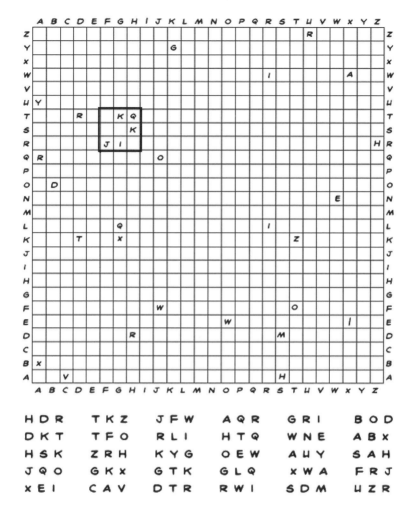

Figure 15: A Herivel Square

The supposition then is that the four closely neighbouring indicators in this box have been contributed by rogue operators and are therefore in the neighbourhood of the *ringstellung* which is then possibly among F, G, H for the left-hand wheel, R, S, T for the middle wheel and I, J, K for the right-hand wheel, giving in all 27 suggested *ringstellung* as opposed to the original 17,576 possible ones!

There must have been some intense discussion between Welchman and myself on how best to set up the Herivel Square physically, and in no time Welchman provided me with a blackboard and easel, and a supply of large sheets of squared paper to be attached to the blackboard by drawing pins. It can be imagined with what enthusiasm and high hopes I first began to look for clusters in various codes around the beginning of March 1940.

Notice *en passant,* how this square explains why the Germans never noticed clusters although they were constantly beneath their eyes: before the 30 indicators in this example are put on the square there is no trace of any clusters, you cannot *see* them, but when they are put on the square in the way indicated you immediately can. But before you can think of using a square in this way you need the whole of my theory of which the Germans fortunately never had any inkling.

Soon after I began to keep the Herivel Square, around 1 March 1940, someone had one of those ideas which are immediately obvious—once seen. Take any Military Enigma code—Army or Air Force—broken by the method of sheets: it will give, among other things, the actual *ringstellung* of the three wheels for the code in question, and this can then be compared with clusters, if any, of the corresponding Herivel Square. The results gradually became increasingly discouraging; during the period 1 March to 30 April there were some 50 such codes broken by the method of sheets, but in no one of these did the corresponding Herivel Square give any sort of striking indication of the correct *ringstellung.*

Apparently, however, this did not deter me from continuing to test the Herivel Square. Why? I have no idea, as I seem to have largely blacked out the whole period from a little after 1 March up to 1 May—repressed it perhaps, as being too painful to remember. Reasons for my perseverance can be found, of course. According to David Rees, I had 'the courage of my convictions'.* Again, as Blaise Pascal famously said "The heart has its reasons which reason does not understand," and against the odds, and against reason, I may simply have felt in my bones that such a beautiful theory—as it must have seemed to me—*must* be right. Also, no matter how may times it failed, that never precluded it from succeeding some other time in the future; *there was always hope*, perhaps the most important reason of all for persevering. Whatever the reason, or reasons, I continued to keep faith with the Herivel Square, and by around the end of April my colleagues must have agreed, tacitly or otherwise—perhaps to humour me—to do likewise when I was not on the night or morning shifts.

*See below, Appendix II (b).

— Chapter 12 —

The Breakthrough:
With its
Momentous Consequences

On lst May 1940, with one totally inexplicable exception, the Germans suddenly dropped all their double encodements in the preface, as a result of which the corresponding Military Enigma codes became unbreakable by the Polish method of sheets: the mysterious exception was the so-called Yellow code of the unsuccessful Norwegian campaign which now continued to be broken every day by the Poles or ourselves. That meant that we were still able to continue to test the Herivel Square every day—but not the Poles, who knew nothing about Herivelismus as they had not been told. So every day my hopes were duly dashed, while at the same time the niggling fear that we would never break any Military Enigma codes other than the Yellow again was ratcheted up a notch or two, especially in Hut 3, who would have probably known or guessed—which we in Hut 6 did not—that the Wehrmacht was poised to strike in the West. But 'if hopes are dupes, fears may be liars', and so it proved.

Soon after 10 May a hitherto unknown phenomenon swam into the ken of the machine-room night shift: one particular area of the Herivel Square of the Red (Luftwaffe) code of the day became ever more densely populated as the indicators of new Red messages poured in from the Registration Room at a rate unprecedented for the Red or any other code before, and possibly after. Ultimately the point must have been reached where the chances of this immensely powerful cluster not being a true bill, of it not containing the *ringstellung* of the day, had became so slim that the members of the night or morning shift, or both, evidently felt impelled to make a leap into the unknown and cast around in the dark for some new way to break Enigma based on the handful of possible *ringstellung* allowed by the Herivel Square of the day.

They were triumphantly successful. When I arrived un-suspecting for tea and the evening shift around 4 p.m. that day, the door to Hut 6 was open, and Gordon Welchman was standing a little to one side as if he was waiting for me, as indeed he was: the master waiting for the pupil, the curious reversal of the event some ten years earlier which silently marked the first step towards Herivelismus, when the pupil was waiting for the master. Welchman explained to me what had happened, and inside in the left-hand corner of the room I could see a group surrounding David Rees—who according to a copy of a letter of mine to Welchman of 11/10/84 given in Appendix II below—'was in the process of completing the break'.

And so in this extraordinary denouement, Herivelismus, which had been conceived around Valentine's Day, saved from oblivion by steady testing over a period of some 10 weeks against codes broken by the Polish method of sheets, had now been delivered by others whose attitude to my theory had changed from scepticism to belief between the morning and the after-noon of this memorable day.

The feeling in the machine room seemed one of shock rather than elation as we all in different ways came to terms with this extraordinary event.

After this first occasion, potentially the most difficult, with no guarantee of repetition, the Red continued to be broken by hand with very few exceptions till sometime in late August or early September. By this time the Turing-Welchman Bombes were coming on stream, although, as Welchman himself emphasised, without the cribs supplied by months of hand-breaking, the Bombes themselves would never have got off the ground.

A brief account of the method of hand-breaking is given later in this chapter. The first hand-break was certainly the most brilliant improvisation in the history of Hut 6, if not of the whole of Bletchley Park. However, some readers may not be so certain that soon after the 10th of May—a day which marked both the onset of the Blitzkrieg in France and the appointment of Churchill as Prime Minister of the United Kingdom of Great Britain and Northern Ireland—was when hand-breaking began in Hut 6, a question to which we shall now turn.

Soon after we had begun to break the Red day by day with the help of massive Herivel Tips, I vividly remember dropping in at Hut 3 next door—where they translated the messages we broke—when work was slack and it was dark, which in May must have been towards the end of the evening shift or the beginning of the night shift, to see how the battle went. The members of Hut 3 seemed to treat me with some deference, and were always very friendly and welcoming, showing me the details of the actual battle front based on the latest decodes, spread out on an immense table covered with maps and lamps with green-coloured shades casting pools of light in the surrounding gloom. One memory stands out with particular clarity as relating to a specific event: an account they gave me, based on one of our decodes, with indication of the actual location on the map, of how amidst the disintegration of defeat a French armoured division had stood its ground against a German Panzer division advancing towards St Quentin.

Some 63 years later, in 2003, when reading up about

the Blitzkrieg, I came across a more detailed account of the same incident in Henri Michel's meticulously documented *Second World War* in which the German commanding officer involved in the skirmish referred to above is given as General Guderian (Fig. 16), seen here in his command vehicle with his radio and Enigma operators and their assistant. It was from this vehicle that the encode of the message in question must have been transmitted to Guderian's immediate superior von Kleist, but not on the Red, on which it would have been retransmitted, intercepted by Chatham, decoded by Hut 6, pushed through the conduit from the Registration Room to Hut 3 next door by the long brush, translated there, and its contents divulged to me later the same night or early the next morning.

Figure 16: General Guderian's command vehicle

As for the commander of the French armoured group, it was given by Michel as Colonel Charles de Gaulle, promoted General the next day for his quixotic bravery. Finally, and fortunately from my point of view, the date of the engagement was given as 16 May, conclusive proof we were breaking the Red by that date. But can we push the date back earlier still? I think we can.

Once we began to break the Red by hand—whenever that was—we continued to do so day by day almost without exception for some three months at least. Compare that with the situation between 1 March and 30 April, in which we broke around 50 codes without a trace of a Herivel Tip. There must, therefore, have been certain characteristics of some of the Red operators after May 1 which were responsible for the daily production of powerful Herivel Tips from at least 16 May onwards and which were missing in the period before hand-breaking. We know what these special characteristics were: they were those of rogue operators who set their *ringstellung* after putting their wheels in the scrambler, and then failed to twiddle their wheels backwards or forwards 'well away from their positions near the poles' (see p 91 above). What possible reason could there be, then, for this group of operators to be present in adequate numbers for some three months on almost every day on and after the 16th, and not to be present on the 15th, or 14th right back to the 10th May? Unless, that is, there was a lull in the fighting in which case there might not have been enough rogue operators to provide a powerful Herivel Tip. But there is no trace whatsoever of such a lull in any of these days in Churchill's account in Volume 2 of his *The Second World War'* (1951 edition), not excluding 10th May itself where he specifically states: 'long before day-break (on 10th May) one hundred and fifty miles of front were aflame.' *

* Churchill, *op. cit.* p. 42.

However, before we decide that the first hand-break of the Red Luftwaffe code was actually on 10 May, we must allow for the possibility of a security black-out of all Enigma messages at the beginning of the Blitzkrieg. According to a private communication from GCHQ: 'On 10 May the Germans invaded Belgium and France, *maintaining radio silence for two days.*' This would imply that the first hand-breaking of the Red Luftwaffe code was on the 12 May. On the other hand, at page 632 of Roy Jenkins' biography of Winston Churchill we find the following: 'Almost the only piece of good news at the beginning of Churchill's premiership was that of an important cryptographic Enigma breakthrough at Bletchley on 11 May', which would imply a black-out of 10 May only. To cover these two possibilities I have used 'soon after 10 May' whenever referring to the first hand-break of the Red code. This has to be compared with the two references to 10 May in my letter of 11 October 1984 to Welchman (see Appendix II).

The hand-breaking of the non-Naval German Military Enigma Luftwaffe code soon after 10 May 1940 was the climax of the campaign against German Military Enigma in the period up to May 1940. Subsequently the Red code was broken daily apart from a handful of gaps until sometime between the end of August and the middle of September when an accumulation of cribs from hand-breaking led to the first success of the Turing-Welchman Bombe. Thereafter, there would have been a daily competition between hand-breaking and Bombe-breaking until the members of the Machine Room in Hut 6 had found a hitherto unbroken code with sufficiently strong Herivel Tips for it to be broken by hand, after which the Red code would have been increasingly taken over by Bombes.

To read a given Military Enigma code on a particular day it was necessary to know the three wheels given in the key of the day, their *ringstellung*, in what order they had been placed on the axle before being fitted into the scrambler, and the stecker. In the case of hand-breaking, the Herivel Tip suggested a greatly restricted number of *ringstellung* out of the initial 17,576 possibilities, while cillis* with the help of the Nigelian method† could reduce the initial 60 possible wheel-orders substantially, even as low as 2. In this latter case, and in the example from Welchman's *The Hut Six Story* given in Chapter 11 where there were 27 different *ringstellung* possibilities, the number of combined *ringstellung*-wheel order possibilities would be 27 x 2 = 54. In general, if there were R probable Herivel Tip *ringstellung* candidates and W probable wheel orders, the number of combined *ringstellung*-wheel order possibilities would be R x W; this was the critical number for hand-breaking, since each of the combined possibilities had to be tested in turn for stecker contradictions by a method described on pp. 104-110 of Welchman's *The Hut Six Story*. But if the number of combined possibilities was too large, say 200 as opposed to 54, then finding the correct candidate or candidates free of stecker contradictions could be an excessively lengthy process, something which might be beyond the inevitably limited time that could be allotted to a given day's messages in the hectic early months of hand-breaking and decoding of the Red to satisfy the insatiable demands of Hut 3 next door.

I shall term the hand-breaking described above as 'direct'. But there was another indirect type of hand-breaking: imagine a code which had originally been broken by hand and then put on the Bombe, and that there was another unbroken code which the 'crib' team

* See Rees' account of cillis at pp. 124-125 below.

† Nigel Foreman of Hut 6 had discovered in the summer of 1940 that on a given day the wheels in the left-hand, middle and right-hand positions in the scrambler were always different from those in the same positions the day before. This automatically reduced the number of possible wheel orders on a given day from 60 to 32.

in Hut 6 under Milner-Barry had reasons for believing was in one way or another related to the first code. In that case they might find a succession of messages on different days on the second code which resembled a certain regularly transmitted crib message on the first code. This could suggest that the second, unbroken, code could carry the same crib, an hypothesis which could then be tested on the Bombe and, if repeatedly successful, the amount of information acquired on new cribs in the second code might be sufficient to put it on the Bombe permanently in its own right. I call this way of putting the second code onto the Bombe an indirect hand-breaking, for although it had been put directly on the Bombe without the preliminary period of hand-breaking, this would have been impossible without the help of the first code which itself had initially depended on hand-breaking.

And so all the 50 or so non-Naval Military codes broken in Hut 6 after 1 May 1940 ultimately depended on *a smaller core of directly hand-broken codes* without which none of them could ever have been put on the Bombe, with the possible exception of those permanently broken as a result of captured monthly key books.

In the Preface, I emphasised that the process of hand-breaking involved factors other than the Herivel Tip. But the latter was always a *necessary* factor: even if on a particular code on a particular day the wheel order had been reduced by 'cillis' to only three possibilities for the left hand wheel—the middle and right hand wheels being known—or even to two possibilities if one of the three had been excluded for Nigelian reasons, no hand-breaking could be contemplated in the absence of a Herivel Tip for the day in question. So that the conclusion reached in the preceding paragraph still remains true if the section in italics is replaced by '*the Herivel Tip*'.

— Epilogue —

The account of hand-breaking in the preceding chapter concluded that the presence of a powerful Herivel Tip was a *necessary* condition for initiating a hand-break. But a Herivel Tip could never be spotted on a given day before a concentrated cluster had appeared somewhere on its Herivel Square, and this square had in turn originally begun to be used—unsuccessfully for some 10 weeks as it turned out—around the beginning of March 1940 as a result of the discovery of the theory of Herivelismus a week or so earlier in February. Thereafter, all hand-breaks on Military Enigma after 30 April 1940 ultimately depended on this theory of Herivelismus. But—as we have seen in Chapter 12—all codes put on the Bombe depended directly or indirectly on hand-breaks. This leads me to the following conclusion: *without the discovery of Herivelismus, no non-Naval Military Enigma codes could have been broken beyond 30 April 1940*—exception, of course, being made of the Yellow code, and any breaking due to the capture of Enigma operators' monthly key books.

In a statement about the Herivel Tip enclosed with a letter of December 1999, my old friend and Machine Room colleague David Rees concluded: 'The Enigma story (in the summer and autumn of 1940) would have been very different without the Herivel Tip'.* Having pondered over David's conclusion from time to time during the last 6½ years I find I would now want to amend it as follows: 'Without the discovery of Herivelismus the story of non-Naval Enigma would have terminated on 30 April 1940 when—with the exception of the Yellow code—the Germans suddenly dropped the double encodement in the preface which they had previously employed in all Military Enigma codes over a period of some 12 years.'

* See Appendix I (b) below, p. 125.

In the spring of 1941 I committed an unfortunate oversight on the prefaces of a long multi-part Enigma message to or from the Afrika Korps shortly after it had begun to arrive in North Africa.

To restore my somewhat battered self-confidence I composed a sonnet commemorating the discovery of February 1940, praying fervently that any delay this oversight might have caused in putting the Afrika-Korps Enigma code on to the Bombe via hand-breaks would be outweighed by the contribution which Herivelismus might already have made to the war effort, above all in the Battle of Britain,* fought out to a draw between the RAF and the Luftwaffe high above in the blue skies of that wonderfully beautiful summer of 1940.

* See Winterbotham, pp 52-4.

Ex Tenebris Lux

I wonder shall I ever know
Beyond these twisted thoughts that grow,
Yet always flicker just below
The burning light of consciousness:

They shout and jostle in my mind,
These words that I can never find,
Or stumble forth, inchoate, blind
In unconvincing argument:

Yet, sometimes, when the mind is still,
With easy unremembered skill,
They flood my sense with sudden thrill,
And purge my soul of every ill,
And banish all my foolish fears,
So swift and free and flowing *clear.*

— End —

—Appendices—

I: Technical Appendix

Consider the letter track of an Enigma wheel as seen, for example, at the right of Figure 4 in Chapter 10. Before the letters could be etched or stuck onto the surface of the track, the latter would have to be divided into 26 equal sectors by a series of *straight* lines (on the curved surface of the track) all perpendicular to the two edges of the track and therefore parallel to each other. Imagine an axle threaded through the inner tube of the wheel and clamped horizontally above a horizontal table. Then withdraw the *ringstellung* bolt and lean over the wheel and turn it round until one is looking straight down on one of the sectors. This sector will then appear somewhat as is in Figure A1, where a, b and c, d are the two parallel lines separating the given sector from the ones on either side. Here e and f are midway between a and d, and b and c respectively. Join e, f by a straight line on the curved surface, and let g be midway between e and f. This (uniquely determined) point g I shall call the 'centre' of the section in question, and the letter etched or stuck onto it will have been 'centred' as far as possible on this point. In the case of some letters, such as X or I, the centring will have been direct and unambiguous; in the case of other letters such as Q or R the craftsmen concerned would simply have had to do the best they could.

I now want to explain how I think the *ringstellung* hole 'opposite' the letter in question must have been drilled in the first place. For this, imagine the following process—necessitated by the near impossibility of seeing any—let alone all—of the *ringstellung* holes because of the 'well' and the serrated disc as in Figure 5 in Chapter 10. Suppose the wheel is immobilised by means of a

110

strut attached to the clamp, that the *ringstellung* apparatus is unscrewed at its fixed end, and that the wheel is then sawn off flush with the right-hand surface of the letter tract, thus removing both the well and the serrated disc.

I now imagine that the remains of the axle on the left-hand side is reclamped in a vertical position, the remnant of the wheel itself being below, and once again prevented from moving by means of a strut attached to the clamp.

If one looks down on the exposed side of the letter track from a point in the line through the centre of the axle, what one sees will be as in Figure A2. The annulus between the two outer circles represents the 'skirt' of the letter track in which the 26 *ringstellung* holes are drilled: the outer ring is the top of the skirt, the first inner ring is its bottom and the adjacent thin annulus is the thickness of the inner *drum** of the wheel which serves a double purpose: (i) it houses the wires connecting the pins on the side of the wheel to the studs on the other end and (ii) it produces a fixed smooth surface on which all of the potentially movable parts of the wheel—including the letter track and the serrated disc—can slide smoothly once the *ringstellung* pin has been withdrawn. The small circle at the centre represents a section of the axial tube through which the axle is threaded.

Finally, I imagine the left hand end of the axle is once again clamped in a horizontal position, and that all the *ringstellung* holes and the central core are filled up with plastic wood and painted over so that an observer stationed at a point on the (imaginary) extension of the axial line—and properly oriented—will have the view shown in Figure A3 below. Here, C is the point at the centre of the central core of Figure A2 representing

* Part of which is the 'well' in Figure 5, p 83.

111

the axle and tube (in other words C is on the *axial* line), c, f and b are the *same* points as in in Figure A1, but whereas *there* they were regarded as being on the *edge* of the sector of the letter track in question, *now* they appear as on the top of a corresponding *sector* c, f, b, i, h of the skirt, the same shape and size as all the 25 other such sectors which together make up the whole surface of the (annular) skirt.

The straight line joining f and C evidently bisects h, i at j, and so divides the sector c, f, b, i, h into two equal parts: by symmetry, or common sense, or both, the point marked by Scherbius or his assistant for drilling the *ringstellung* hole 'corresponding to' or 'opposite' the centre 'g' of the letter X, say, actually on the sector in question, must have been somewhere on the line f, j, not too close to either f or j. I have marked this point arbitrarily at k, and all of the other 25 identical sectors of the skirt will have their *ringstellung*-hole drilling points at the same distance C k from the centre of the circle on which they lie. I have thus characterised uniquely the centres 'g' and corresponding *ringstellung* points 'k' of the letter track and skirt. And when I say (in Chapter 11) that the *ringstellung* pin is 'opposite' a letter on the track, 'opposite' is taken to mean the relationship between a 'g' and a 'k' as above, where the drilling point k in question will actually be at the centre of the mouth of the corresponding *ringstellung* hole.

It remains to bring in the (vital) notion of pole points. If the remnant of the wheel is now freed so that it can rotate freely round its horizontal axis, every point of it will describe a circle with centre somewhere on the axial line and in a plane perpendicular to it. In the case of the line e, f in Figure A1, since it is perpendicular to the two edges of the wheel track it will be parallel to the axial line. This means that these two lines will lie on a plane, and as the wheel rotates clockwise, say, as viewed from the right, each of the points on this plane will sweep out equal angles round the particular circles on which they lie, and so all of them will reach their pole-positions on their circles simultaneously, or, to put it another way, the angular distance from g, say, along its circle before it reaches its pole-position—i.e. its maximum height above its centre on the axial line—will be equal to the angular distance of any other point on the said plane. But if one looks at the line f, j, C, since one point f is on the line g, f of Figure A1 and another point C is on the axial line, then the whole line f, j, C is on the 'rotation' plane joining e, g, f to the axial line. Therefore all the points on the line f, j, C will be at the same distance from their pole points. Therefore the 'drilling point' k will be at the same angular distance from its pole point as the 'centre' g will be from its pole point. This result, together with the exact meanings of the oppositeness to the 'centre' of a letter track sector, and the 'position' of a *ringstellung* hole, clear up all the lacunae noted in Chapter 11, pp 95-96.

Figure A1

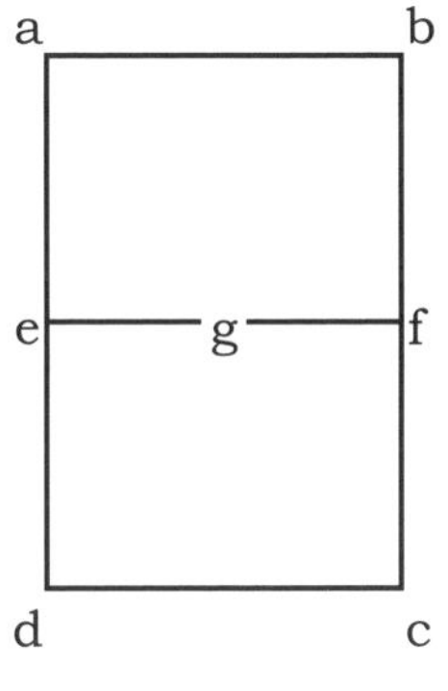

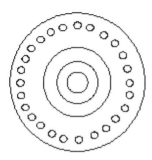

Figure A2

Figure A3

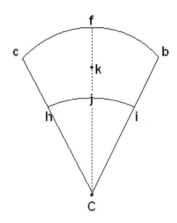

II: Historical Appendix

(a) Welchman – Herivel Correspondence of 1984

1. Letter from Welchman to Herivel of 20 September 1984

Dear John,

I am writing to ask if you can tell me when Jeffreys and his team came to Hut 6 and started using his perforated sheets there; also when you thought of the Herivel Tip. The reason is that in July I was asked by Robin Denniston of the Oxford University Press to write a paper on the early days at Bletchley Park. I want to discuss how things got started and how much depended on what happened during the first two years, September 1939 to September 1941.

Last month, to get background on the Polish contribution, I read a new article by Stengers, "Enigma, the French, the Poles and the British, 1931-1940" which has recently been published in England as part of "The Missing Dimension" (Macmillan), and a new book, "Enigma", by Kozaczuk, which contains as appendices writings of Rejewski which were first published in America in 1982; too late to be used in my book, which went to press in summer 1981. I have also made contact with Lisicki, who was intimately associated with Rejewski.

Lisicki has convinced me that the collaboration between Bletchley and Rejewski's team at Bruno was agreed in London in December 1939, that Turing took a set of Jeffreys sheets to Bruno on 17 January 1940, and that the exchange of broken keys started immediately. I knew nothing about this at the time, but it now seems that several breaks were made in the Cottage before Jeffreys came to Hut 6. I hope to get information about these breaks from Peter Twinn.

Lisicki has a complete list of keys broken at Bruno and Bletchley between 17 January and 21 June 1940, which will help. But to sort things out I want to fix the date at which breaks began to be made in Hut 6, rather than at the Cottage. I have already written to Reg Parker, and am now writing to David Rees and John Chamberlain* I hope that, between the four of you, you will be able to remember. My own guess is that it could have been as late as early March.

I would also like to know when you arrived at Bletchley Park, and whether you worked in the Cottage before coming to Hut 6. If you did, please tell me what was going on. Babbage tells me that when he arrived in the Cottage around Christmas 1939, they were already working on Cillis, which surprises me.

Did you invent the Herivel Tip before Turing's visit to Bruno on 17 January 1940? I hope so, because this would explain how the Poles came to know about it. If not, perhaps you know when the Poles were told. It seems unlikely that the Poles thought of it themselves, because it is not mentioned in any of Rejewski's writings. Lisicki has told me of a "Knox Method" that was known after May 1940 at Cadix and involved your Tip.

Incidentally Dennis Babbage wrote to me a long time ago to point out that what I said about Sillies in my book was utterly wrong. He gave me a description of the principle of Cillis, which he has recently improved. I am hoping to get permission to publish it.

A lot of errors in my book will have to be corrected in what I am now writing. For example I now know how the Bomba worked and what it was designed to do. Our bombe was not developed from the Bomba. It contained

---

* This is an error by Welchman. Chamberlain's first name was 'Malcolm'.

116

five new ideas which, Lisicki confirms, were not known to Rejewski.

I hope you are flourishing. I am doing well on two total hip replacements, a pacemaker, and pills. I "retired" in 1971, but went on doing consulting work until 1982. This was mainly concerned with problems of military communications, intelligence, and security. It is a pleasant change to get back to thinking about the early days at Bletchley.

I will be most grateful for your help. If you are interested, I will ask Robin Denniston to show you a preliminary draft.

Yours,

Gordon Welchman

2. Letter from Herivel to Welchman of 11 October 1984

Dear Gordon,

I was very pleasantly surprised to get your letter and find how intellectually fit and active you are in spite of 'two hip replacements, a pacemaker and pill' which sounds rather fearsome. I am myself pretty fit and so far have no need for any advanced technological aids. I retired early in 1979 and came to live in Oxford. Not the most bracing of places, but near good country in the Cotswolds and of course well served with all sorts of facilities. Also I was a visiting fellow at All Souls in 1978 and this has given me some dining rights there in the last 5 years which have been a source of stimulation and pleasure.

Now to your questions: I cannot tell you when Jeffreys and his team came to Hut 6, it was certainly before my time. I came on 29 January 1940, following a visit you paid me at Sidney. David Rees had already come, and I'm pretty sure Malcolm Chamberlain came at the same time as me. I went straight to Hut 6, was never in the Cottage.

As regards the Herivel Tip, or Herivelismus as Kendrick used to call it, thank you for being so flattering about it in your book, which I much enjoyed incidentally, and over which belated congratulations, but you didn't get it quite right as far as the origin of my idea. On page 98 you say "Herivel's attention was drawn to a quirk in machine set-up practice". In fact it was quite different. Once I had got the hang of the Enigma machine early in February 1940, I found myself continually thinking how one could find a way of breaking into it, a pretty good indication that the code was not being broken with any frequency if at all at that period, but I confess I cannot enlighten you about that. Then one evening in my digs I had a brain wave. I was imagining an operator setting up his machine for the day when suddenly a thought struck me that if he were lazy, or in a great hurry he might not turn his wheels much if after setting the Ringstellung of the day, and if he then went on to use the letters appearing in the windows as those of the indicator setting in the preamble of his first message, the latter would be close to the Ringstellung itself. At that time of course, I did not know that German operators had explicit instructions not to do this. When I related this idea to colleagues including yourself it was immediately recognised as a possible way into the Enigma, and you then detailed me off to look for clustering in early messages in a given day. But my recollection is that there was nothing very striking before the German Blitzkrieg on 10th May when suddenly a number of operators forgot themselves and the neighbourhood of the Ringstellung of the day stood out with unmistakable clarity, as a result of which the Red of the day was broken by hand by David

Rees. I remember this very vividly because when I came in on the afternoon shift David was in the process of completing the break in [and] you yourself told me what happened and promised I wouldn't be forgotten.

From what I have said you will see that I did not have the idea of the Ringstellung before Turing's visit to Bruno of Jan 19th 1940. Also as the idea remained hypothetical before May 10th when it was given the first, vital confirmation (for the first break led to the first cribs later) it is extremely unlikely that the Poles could have learnt of it before then. How they got to know of it I do not know but the fact that a "Knox Method" known to the Poles at Cadiz* after May 1940 involved my Tip would seem to point strongly to that being one source of their knowledge. Incidentally I am flabbergasted to hear that such top secret information was passed to the Poles in Cadiz* at that time. But then Dilly was, I am sure, a potential security risk given his totally vague personality.

I hope I have now answered all the queries in your letter.

One final point, I should be interested to see a preliminary draft of Robin Denniston's but if it came between May and August ask Robin to ring me first, and if he could get no reply send it to me at Belval Bourg, 50210 Cerisy-la-Salle, France, our summer hide-out.

Best wishes,

Yours,

John Herivel

---

* 'Cadiz' is an error for 'Cadix' in the French unoccupied zone during the first three years of the Second World War.

3. Letter from Welchman to Herivel of 6 December 1984

Dear John,

Your letter of October 11 was very interesting and helpful. After a lot of hard work I sent a hand-written preliminary draft to Denniston on 6 November. Then Lisicki sent me the record that Langer kept of Enigma breaks exchanged between Bletchley and Bruno. It is fascinating, and made me decide to write another chapter, which I sent to Denniston three days ago. The title and contents are now:

From Polish Bomba to British Bombe: The Birth of Ultra
> *The Poles, The British and The French*
> *The Critical Six Months   August 1939 to January 1940*
> *The First Two Years August 1939 to July 1941*
> *Causes of Confusion*
> *Rejewski's Brilliant Cryptanalysis*
> *Dilly Knox and Bruno*
> *The Bombe was NOT All That Mattered*
> *Langer's List of 126 Broken Enigma Keys*
>> *Illustrations and Tables*
>> *Chronological List of References*

Please regard this information as confidential until the material has been shown to the authorities.

Denniston has already sent me a typewritten version of chapters 1 to 7, which required remarkably little correction, but the whole thing will not be in presentable shape until early January, after which there will be a period of editing, during which I hope you will give me your comments.

The Langer list has helped me to pin down when things happened. It fits in with your memory, in that there were no breaks between January 5 and February 8 of 1940. Apart from the last pre-war break, the list starts with breaks achieved around January 17 when Turing took the sheets to the Poles. The sudden effectiveness of the Herivel Tip around May 20 shows up very clearly, as does the fact that this change of indicating system was made on May 15, not on May 10 as has been generally accepted. (The Germans had made two earlier changes on the 15th day of a month). It now looks as if 24-hour operations of the Registration Room and Control Room started at the end of December 1939 and that Jeffreys and his people moved from the Cottage to Hut 6 between January 17 and January 22. I am still hoping that Reg Parker and David Rees will fix these two dates, but they have not yet answered my letters.

Winterbotham caused confusion by saying that we started breaking Enigma early in April. Ronald Lewin in "Ultra goes to War", repeated this error and gave the impression that we did not start 24 hour operation until around the time of Hitler's invasion of Denmark and Norway. Hinsley in his "Official History" repeated both these errors (and added a lot more).

The Langer list contains a clue to the mysterious Yellow key that, according to Hinsley, was introduced by the German Army for the Norwegian campaign. The list shows that, with the exception of April 13, Red was broken every day from April 8 to May 14, and Red was undoubtedly used for Army/Air coordination. But on seven days, April 9, 10, 19, 21, 22, 23 and 25, a second key was broken. This would have been the Yellow key used exclusively by the Army. I don't remember anything about this. Do you?

> *Best wishes for Christmas*
> *And New Year*
>
> *Gordon*

P.S. According to Hinsley (vol 2, page 662) the first break of Yellow was made on April 10, 1940. This could well have been the key for April 9.

(b) The Herivel Tip
Enclosed with a letter from David Rees of 1999

This is an account of John Herivel's brilliant idea which came to be known as the Herivel Tip, considering, in particular, its role in leading to the continuous breaking of the Luftwaffe Enigma keys from 1940 onwards. I will only give a brief description of the Tip itself, since I cannot improve on John's own account in "Station X", except in one respect. I do not recollect being the person who was responsible for the first successful use of the Tip in breaking a day's key. In fact, my recollection is of returning from leave to go onto night shift, and being told that it had happened. Since this all happened 59 years ago, it is possible that my memory is at fault. First, some history. Howard Smith (later head of MI5) and myself were the first two of Gordon Welchman's tutorial students to be recruited to work on Enigma. This was in December 1939, and we were followed in February 1940 by John Herivel and Malcolm Chamberlain. The four of us became later founder members of the Machine room run by John Jeffreys and were responsible for the testing of the results which were produced by the Netze, the method used to break Enigma at that time. Initially, we were breaking old keys. It was during this period that John had the idea that, if we looked at the indicators of the initial messages sent out by individual operators, these would be close to the ringstellung as he has explained in the book "Station X". The idea was not borne out by the old keys we broke nor, when we were breaking the Yellow key used in Norway in April 1940 by the keys of that cipher. Fortunately, John had the courage of his convictions, and he continued to make a daily analysis [on the Herivel Square].

On I believe, May 1st 1940, the Germans changed the method of sending the machine setting for messages, and this meant that the Netze could no longer be used. We had to find a method of breaking daily keys by hand, to bridge the gap until the bombes became available, and, incidentally, break traffic over a period of months to be able to recognise the regular messages which could be used as cribs, to run on the bombes. This was a tall order. Fortunately for us, the German training of their cipher clerks was abysmal, and under pressure, there were widespread errors in cipher security. This became apparent from the invasion of Holland and Belgium onwards.

The first mistake made by many cipher clerks was at the beginning of the day when they had to choose three of the five available rotors, insert them in the correct order in the machine and then, on each of these three rotors insert a clip in a hole on the collar which carried the letters A to Z. There were, on each collar, 26 holes, one opposite each letter. The holes chosen on the three rotors were those opposite the three letters of the ringstellung for the day. The natural way to insert the clips with the rotors already in the machine left the letters of the ringstellung showing in the windows when the lid was closed (or, at least, letters close to them in the alphabet) and if they did not move the wheels before enciphering the first message, the external indicator of the first message which is sent in clear would be close to the ringstellung. This would show up by external indicators of first messages forming a cluster and gave us a reasonable guess that the ring-stellung was near the centre of the cluster. This was the Herivel Tip. It is curious to think that if only the clips had been put in the holes before the rotors were put in the machine, the Herivel Tip wouldn't have worked.

The second mistake was similar. A cipher clerk had often to encipher a string of messages one after the other, particularly, multipart messages. He had to choose, for each message, the settings of the three rotors at which the encipherment of the message should start. This is the internal indicator. This was not sent in clear, instead he chose a second set of three letters, called the external indicator, moved the three rotors so that these letters showed through the windows and then enciphered the chosen interior indicator. What was then sent in clear was the exterior indicator followed by the encipherment of the interior indicator. A clerk could save time in enciphering a string of messages, if when ending one message, he looked at the windows and chose what he read as the exterior indicator of the next part. He could then encipher the interior indicator at this setting without moving the rotors. Of course he then had to move the rotors before enciphering the next message. This form of laziness was very common, and had been spotted by the Poles before the war. In conjunction with a second mistake this was disastrous. If one assumed the above had taken place, it was possible to work back from the external indicator of one message and obtain a small number of possibilities for the interior indicator of the previous message. The possibilities depended which rotors were in the machine. If in a multipart message we obtained a string of possible interior indicators which showed some sort of pattern, for example QAY, WSX, EDC, RFV, TGB, ZHN which are diagonally across the keyboard of the enigma machine, we would assume that we were dealing with a lazy operator. We would then have information about which rotors occupied which positions in the machine and a number of three letter cribs known as cillis. This would not have been enough without the Herivel Tip. The two together were sufficient for the members of the machine room to break the main Luftwaffe cipher on a daily basis for the rest of the summer and autumn of 1940. By this time the bombes were becoming available and the group responsible for finding cribs had done their work, so that, when the German signal security was tightened up, the use of the Herivel Tip and cillis became less important, though when new keys were introduced, they did make a comeback, particularly in the North African Theatre. In fact, the members of the machine room were eventually *transferred to work with the crib room, and together they formed the watch. Some of us, John Herivel, Keith Batey, and myself included, transferred to other parts of Bletchley Park.*

Without the Herivel Tip and cillis the Enigma cipher would not have broken at all, let alone on a regular basis, during the summer and autumn of 1940. Apart from the contribution that the breaking of the Enigma may have made to the Battle of Britain, we would not have been able to recognise the pattern of regular messages which could be used as cribs. The Enigma story would have been very different without the Herivel Tip.

(c) Churchill's Visit
[End of lecture on Herivelismus given at Sidney Sussex College, Cambridge, on 9 October 2005]

In the Autumn of 1941 the Prime Minister paid a surprise visit to Bletchley Park. Word suddenly reached us in Hut 6 that he was coming, and those in the Machine Room—of whom I was still a member—were told to stand up facing their machines. People were much more biddable in those days, so we did what we were told and for what seemed an eternity waited patiently. Then the sound of many voices was heard in the distance, gradually becoming louder and louder and reaching a crescendo immediately behind me before subsiding when Welchman's voice was heard saying 'Sir, I would like to present John Herivel who was responsible for breaking the German Enigma last year.' On hearing my name spoken by Welchman in this totally unexpected manner I turned automatically to the right to find myself gazing straight into the eyes of the Prime Minister! We looked silently at each other for a moment or two before he moved on surrounded by his entourage. If I had had the necessary presence of mind—which I did not—I would have reminded him that the day the Military Enigma was broken was soon after that on which he himself had become Prime Minister.*

But that was not the end of the matter. After lunch, an hour or two later, we were surprised to hear that Churchill wanted to see everyone again. This time all staff on duty in Huts 3, 6 and 8 were told to gather immediately behind Hut 6 where there was a mound of builders' spoil over which the grass had grown. We were asked to form a semicircle around it—at a respectful distance—so that as many people as possible would see the Prime Minister. Soon he came and scrambled onto the mound where he stood rather uneasily for a moment—for it was a miserably dark day with a cold wind. We saw before us a rather frail, oldish looking man, a trifle bowed, with wispy hair, in a black pin-striped suit with a faint red line, no bravado, no large black hat, no cigar. Then he spoke very briefly, but with deep emotion, on the lines of : "I want to thank you all for what you have done for the war effort". That was *our* finest hour at Bletchley Park. The bitter disappointment of those who were on other shifts can be imagined.

To return to my presentation to Churchill. Why had Welchman made it? For obvious reasons you might say, since a powerful *ringstellung* Tip had been a prerequisite of all hand-breakings of the Red Luftwaffe code after 10 May 1940 until the Turing-Welchman Bombes came on stream the following August or early September. But there was, I fancy, another reason: when Welchman told me on the afternoon of 10 May how the

* See above, Chapter 12.

Red had been broken, he added in a lower tone of voice: "Herivel, this will not be forgotten." The presentation to Churchill could be regarded as the beginning of his 'not forgetting', something which he then elaborated on in his *The Hut Six Story* some 40 years later. Of course he was right, as he usually was, about the *ringstellung* not being forgotten. But there is something else not to be forgotten. Although Welchman and I were normally never 'close' to each other, for there was what was in those days an unbridgeable gap of 12 years between the junior and the senior, nevertheless we did come momentarily very close indeed on, and soon after, that critical moment in the history of Hut 6—and indeed of the War itself—when he unhesitatingly gave an enthusiastic welcome to my new theory, and showed his confidence in it soon afterwards by having prefaces sent up early from Chatham. Without this powerful backing Herivelismus would inevitably have withered away like the flowers of the forest. There would then have been nothing either to remember or forget, and it is not clear how any further Red Luftwaffe or other Military Enigma Codes—apart from the short-lived Yellow—would have been broken from 30 April 1940 onwards for the rest of the war in Europe*. So *Floreat Welchmani Memoriam!*

* See Chapter 12 and Epilogue above.

Gordon Welchman

—Notes—

All references to authors below are to the first names of the full citations of their works in the bibliography of source material below. There are no notes beyond Chapter 8.

Chapter 1: In the Beginning (pp. 13-15)

The authors who have written about the origins of Enigma—Calvocoressi, Garlinski, Kahn, and Lewin—all talk about the Dutchman Hugo Alexander Koch, and the German Arthur Scherbius as being variously involved in what the former termed 'a secret writing machine' and what later became known as 'Enigma'. Calvocoressi (p. 23) states that 'the original version of the Enigma Machine was invented and patented in Holland', Garlinski (pp. 9-10) mentions Koch but hedges his bets as regards priority between him and Scherbius concentrating instead on a detailed account of the development of the Enigma machine by the latter: according to Bauer, Kahn refers to Hugo Koch filing for a patent of a secret writing machine in October 1919 but fails to mention at this point that Arthur Scherbius had already filed for a patent of a rotor machine in 1918; finally, although Lewin (p. 25) mentions Koch's patent of 1918 he declares Scherbius to be 'the true pioneer' of the Enigma machine. However it seems to me that the question of priority between Koch and Scherbius cannot be decided without taking account of Bauer's paper: 'An Error in the History of Rotor Encryption Devices' in *Cryptologia*, Vol. 23 (3). To my way of thinking, Bauer provides conclusive evidence that Scherbius developed the notion of 'rotor machine encryption' independently of Koch, having filed for his own German patent in 1918 before Koch's Dutch patent of 7 October 1919, and for that reason I have made no mention of Koch and have regarded Scherbius as the true inventor of the machine which he then went on to construct and commercialise as the Scherbius Commercial Enigma. This is further reinforced by the fact that although Kahn (1967) makes very little reference to Enigma, or either Koch or Scherbius, Kahn (1991) makes no reference to Koch but gives a great deal of invaluable evidence in chapter 3 about Scherbius. This leads me to conclude that the case in favour of his having been the 'true pioneer' of Enigma, as Lewin (p25) puts it, is overwhelming, and that the title of Chapter 1 of this present work: 'In the Beginning: the Commercial Enigma of Arthur Scherbius' is fully justified. I do not believe that de Leeuw's paper: 'Dutch invention of the rotor machine, 1915-1923.' *Cryptologia*, Vol 27 (1), Jan 2003, affects this conclusion.

1. All the information—including quotations—about Scherbius in this paragraph is taken from Garlinski, pp. 9-10.
2. This paragraph is entirely based on Foss, pp. 43-44. The pages referred to are taken from the reproduction of Foss's original MS (NA HW25/10) in *Action This Day*, pp. 43-46. However, the reference at the end of the paragraph to Travis having bought a portable Enigma in Berlin 'in 1920 or 1921' comes not from the reproduction of Foss's original MS but from a note on the MS itself in the NA from Foss to Nigel de Grey in which the former states that Edward Travis had told him (Foss) that he had bought a portable Enigma machine in Berlin in '1920 or 21 or possibly later'.
3. See Lewin, p. 25, for the first part of the paragraph.
4. Foss, p. 43 and p. 44.
5. Garlinski, p. 9.
6. For Knox's purchase see inset on unsteckered Enigma in Foss, p. 44.
7. Garlinski, p. 10.
8. For this whole paragraph see Garlinski, pp. 9-10.
9. Up to this point the paragraph draws heavily on Garlinski, pp. 3-6.
10. For the first transmission of Reichswehr Enigma see Note 1 of Chapter 2 below.
11. Garlinski, p. 14, for reasons of French awareness.

Chapter 2: Mathematicians Fluent in German (pp. 16-21)

1. Rejewski, p. 246, where the page numbers here and in all subsequent references to Rejewski are to those from Appendix D of Kozaczuk, in my opinion the best of the accounts given to that author by Rejewski. The date 15

July 1928 for the first report of Enigma traffic by Polish monitoring stations gains unexpected—and I think decisive—credence from Bertrand, p. 31, where he quotes an Asché document which cites the period *15 July 1928 to 11 May 1930* as the first in which Reichswehr was associated with an Enigma machine.

2. The account which follows is given by Garlinski, pp. 2-3 who had it from Ludomir Danilewicz, one of the two employees of the AVA Engineering Company who examined the contents of the crate. Rejewski, p. 246, gives much the same account as Danilewicz but dates it to late 1927 or early 1928 instead of the latter's more precise 'beginning of January 1929'.

3. Rejewski, p. 247.

4. See Christopher Andrew, in *Action this Day*, p. 9.

5. Rejewski, p. 247.

6. The answer to this question might be found in a book on Herman Pokorny by Albert Petho, Graz 1998.

7. Rejewski, p. 247.

8. Denniston (1), p.2.

9. The fact that Langer was *'d'essence autrichienne'* (Bertrand, p. 38)—which Bertrand found very convenient when he went to Warsaw in 1931 with the first Asché documents—and the relationship between Francisci Pokorny and Captain Herman Pokorny, said by Rejewski to be the outstanding Austrian Army cryptologist during World War I, raises the question of an Austrian influence on the Polish Cipher Board. On Bertrand's visit to Warsaw in 1931 he also met a certain Colonel Stefan Mayer who according to Garlinski (p. 42), chaired the opening meeting of the tripartite Conference between the Poles, French and British at Warsaw in July 1939, and was at that time the head of Polish Military Intelligence. According to Garlinski again, Mayer had helped Marshal Pilsudski in the war between the Poles and Bolshevik Russians in 1919/20 by breaking ciphers between the Red Army and its political masters. There seems therefore to have been an Austrian influence in the Polish Cipher Board which went back at least to 1929—when we first hear of Langer—by which time Mayer was almost certainly already head of Intelligence at Polish Army Headquarters.

I relate these facts, not to belittle in any way the Polish role in the Polish Cipher Bureau, for it was the Poles who were to break Enigma while Francisci Pokorny, Langer and Mayer played no more than enabling roles in that extraordinary achievement, but out of historical interest, and the piquancy of a situation in which the break-up of the Austro-Hungarian Empire in 1918 freed at least two of its citizens—Mayer and Langer—to find a new and very important role for themselves—against Germany!—by migrating to Warsaw to strengthen—if not to found—the Polish Cipher Bureau with the help of Francisci Pokorny, who from the low German form of his Christian name looks as if he too may have been Austrian, at least on his father's side.

10. Rejewski, p. 247.

Chapter 3: Strange Bedfellows (pp. 22-29)

Apart from certain references to the books by Bertrand, Garlinski, Navarre and Sebag-Montefiore—whose brilliant work of 2000 on Enigma first drew my attention to the German traitor Schmidt—this chapter is based on extracts from Paillole's *Notre Espion chez Hitler* relating to Schmidt, his spy master Lemoine, and Gustave Bertrand the then head of Section D of the Deuxième Bureau of French Army H.Q., especially the riveting verbal accounts given by Lemoine and Bertrand to Paillole in 1936 some four years after their first meetings with Schmidt in November 1931.

1. Sebag-Montefiore, p. 9.
2. Apart from note 1, this paragraph is based on Lemoine's account to Paillole of his first meeting with Schmidt on 1 November 1931 (Paillole, pp. 21–25).
3. Sebag-Montefiore, p.16.
4. Paillole, p. 24.
5. Navarre, pp. 54-56 relates how Asché never concealed his constant need for money lost on gambling.
6. The whole of the above paragraph is based on Paillole, pp. 21-25.
7. Paillole, p. 27.
8. Paillole, p. 27, also footnote 1 on the same page.

9. It should be emphasised that Section D did not deal with cryptology *per se*. There was a separate section for this in French Army Headquarters.
10. See Garlinski, pp. 13-14 for some interesting light on Bertrand's interest in Reichswehr Enigma.
11. The account of Lemoine given up to this point in the present paragraph—including the quotation—is based on Paillole, p. 29, and was given to him by a Commander de Robien whom he (Paillole) was soon to succeed as head of the German section of French Counter-Intelligence. As such, he would have been—*inter alia*—responsible for the security of Lemoine, sometimes referred to by his code-name 'Rex'. Lemoine was arrested by the Abwehr and ultimately made a confession in March 1943 which included an account of the information the French had received from Asché (see Sebag-Montefiore p244, and ibid pp 245-248 for a touching account of Asché's death from cyanide poison which his daughter had maneged to smuggle into his prison at Gestapo headquarters in Berlin).
12. Navarre, p. 72.
13. Bertrand, p. 35.
14. For above paragraph see Paillole, pp. 27-28.
15. See Paillole, pp. 21-25 for details of meeting of 1 November 1931 between Schmidt and Lemoine.
16. Paillole, p. 34.
17. Ibid.
18. Ibid.
19. Ibid.
20. Paillole, p. 35.
21. Paillole, p. 38.
22. Ibid.
23. Ibid.
24. Paillole, p. 39.
25. Bertrand, p. 37.
26. Paillole, p. 40.

Chapter 4: The Little Room Above the Saxon Square (pp. 30-40)

1. Rejewski, p. 247.

2. Rejewski, p. 251.
3. Rejewski, p. 262.
4. Rejewski, p. 263.
5. Rejewski, p. 264.
6. Rejewski, p. 264.
7. Rejewski, p. 265.
8. For an account of these two methods see pp. 14-16 and pp. 17-22 of Carter, Frank: *The first Breaking of Enigma,* Bletchley Park Trust Report Number 10, July 1999.
9. Rejewski, p. 268.
10. Rejewski, p. 269.

Chapter 5: The Years Between (pp. 41-47)

1. Bertrand, p. 36.
2. Bertrand, p. 56.
3. Paillole, p. 39.
4. Christopher Andrew, in *Action This Day*, p. 5.
5. Winterbotham, p. 12.
6. Denniston (2), pp. 49-50.
7. Foss, p. 45.
8. Michael Smith, in *Action This Day*, p. 42.
9. Bertrand, p. 56.
10. Ibid
11. Foss, p. 45.
12. Rejewski, p. 258.
13. Foss, p. 46.
14. Paillole, p. 39.
15. Bertrand, p. 56.
16. Bertrand, p. 57.
17. Ibid.
18. Ibid.
19. Ibid.
20. Ibid.

Chapter 6: Touch and Go (pp. 48-56)

1. For 'rather uncertain' read 'only fair'. Denniston, p2.
2. Foss p 45. His account continues down to the end of the paragraph.
3. See Chap 4 above.

4. Foss, p 45.
5. Bertrand, p 58,
6. National Archives 25/12
7. Denniston, p 3.
8. Bertrand, p 58.
9. Denniston, p 3.
10. Bertrand, p 59.
11. Lewin, p 44.
12. Denniston, p3.
13. See above—note 9 to Chapter 2.
14. Garlinski, p42 above *passim.*
15. Denniston, p 4.
16. Ibid.
17. Bertrand, p 60.
18. Denniston, p 4.
19. Denniston, p 5.
20. Ibid.
21. Ibid.
22. Denniston, p 6.
23. Ibid.
24. Ibid
25. Garlinski, p 56.
26. Bertrand, p 69.

Chapter 7: Honouring Promises (pp. 57-64)

1. Letter of Denniston, 3 August 1939 (NA HW25/12)
2. Letter of Denniston, 31 July 1939 (NA HW25/12)
3. Letter of Bertrand, 11 August 1939 (NA HW25/12)
4. Account given below of Victoria Station meeting from Bertrand, pp. 60-61.
5. Winterbotham, p. 14.
6. Welchman, p. 11.
7. Memorandum of 1 November 1939 (NA HW14/2)
8. Communication from Knox, 28 December 1939 (NA HW14/2)
9. Note from Knox, 7 January 1940 (NA HW25/2)
10. Letter from Menzies, 10 January 1940 (NA HW14/3)
11. *Inter alia*, in an undated note from Bertrand to Knox —in reply to a note from Knox to Bertrand of 7 Feb 1940, (NA

HW25/12)—the latter learns that Enigma was broken (in Bruno) at the first wheel order tried on the 18 January (1940), thus confirming the date of 17 January for Turing's visit to France.

12. Hinsley, F.H. *et al. British Intelligence in the Second World War* Vol 3, pt 2 Appendix 30, p. 952.
13. de Grey, Nigel, 'History of Sigint', p. 90 (NA HW3/95).

Chapter 8: The Exile (pp. 65-73)

1. Welchman, p. 52.
2. Welchman, p. 35.
3. Welchman, p. 37.
4. Welchman, p. 54.
5. Ibid.
6. Ibid.
7. Welchman, p. 55.
8. Welchman, p. 56.
9. Welchman p. 71.
10. Welchman, p. 73.
11. NA HW25/12
12. Welchman, p. 73.
13. Welchman, pp. 74-76.
14. Welchman, p. 76.
15. NA HW 14/2.
16. NA HW 25/12.
17. Denniston to Knox, 11 Nov 1941 (NA HW14/22).
18. Welchman, pp. 81-82. Various other references to the diagonal board will be found in *The Hut Six Story*, which also includes, as an appendix, 'The Bombe with a Diagonal Board'.

— Sources —

Published sources

Andrew, Christopher. 'Bletchley Park in Pre-War Perspective' in Erskine & Smith. *Action This Day.* pp1-14.

Bauer, Friedrich L. 'An Error in the History of Rotor Encryption Devices'. *Cryptologia,* Vol 23 (3), July 1999, pp 206-210.

Bertrand, Gustave. *Enigma ou la plus grande Énigme de la guerre 1939-1945.* [Paris: Plon, 1973].

Budiansky, Stephen. *Battle of Wits: the complete story of code-breaking in World War II.* [London: Viking, 2000].

Calvocoressi, Peter. *Top Secret Ultra.* [London: Cassell, 1980]. Revised edn: Cleobury Mortimer: Baldwin, 2001.

Denniston, Alastair. 'The Government Code and Cypher School between the Wars'. *Intelligence and National Security.* Vol 1 (1), 1986, pp 48-70.

Erskine, Ralph, & Smith, Michael. *Action This Day.* (London: Bantam, 2001).

Foss, Hugh. 'Reminiscences on Enigma' in Erskine & Smith. *Action This Day.* pp 41-6.

Garliński, Józef. *Intercept: the Enigma war.* [London: Dent, 1979].

Hinsley, F H, *et al British Intelligence in the Second World War.* (vols 1 - 3). London: HMSO, 1979-1988.

Kahn, David. *The Codebreakers: the story of secret writing.* [London: Macmillan, 1967]. Revised edn: New York: Scribner, 1996.

Kahn, David. *Seizing the Enigma: the race to break the German U-Boat codes, 1939-1943.* [London: Souvenir, 1992; Boston, Mass.: Houghton, Mifflin, 1991].

Kozaczuk, Wladyslaw. *Enigma: how the German machine cipher was broken.* [London: Arms & Armour, 1984].

Lewin, Ronald. *Ultra Goes to War: the secret story.* [London: Hutchinson, 1978].

Navarre, Henri. *Le Service Renseignements 1871-1944.* [Paris: Plon, 1978].

Paillole, Paul. *Notre Espion Chez Hitler.* [Paris: Laffont, 1985].

Rejewski, Marian. 'Appendix D: How the Polish Mathematicians broke Enigma' in Kozaczuk. *Enigma.* pp 246-271.

Sebag-Montefiore, Hugh. *Enigma: the battle for the code.* [London: Weidenfeld & Nicolson, 2000].

Welchman, Gordon. *The Hut Six Story: breaking the Enigma codes.* [London: Allen Lane, 1982]. Revised edn: Cleobury Mortimer: Baldwin, 1997.

Winterbotham, Frederick W. *The Ultra Secret.* [London: Weidenfeld & Nicolson, 1974].

A valuable bibliography of books and articles on Military Enigma between 1967 and 1984 is given on pages 107-108 of Gordon Welchman's article 'From Polish Bomba to British Bombe: the birth of Ultra' in *Intelligence and National Security*, Vol 1, pt (1), January 1986. The paper, and its bibliography, are reproduced in their entirety in the revised edition of *The Hut Six Story*, published by M & M Baldwin.

Unpublished sources

Material from the National Archive at Kew is cited as NA, and came from the following HW files: 3/95, 14/2, 14/3, 14/22, 25/2, 25/10, 25/12 and 43/70-72, in particular:

Denniston, Alastair. 'How news was brought from Warsaw at the end of July 1939'. NA HW25/12, pp1-6.

Grey, Nigel de. 'History of Sigint'. NA HW3/95.

Milner-Barry, P S., *et al.* 'History of Hut 6'. NA HW43/70, 71, 72.

—Index —

This covers pages 10 - 128.
Illustrations are indicated in **bold**.

*Those who have enjoyed this book might appreciate our other
books on similar subjects . . .*

The Hut Six Story (978-0-947712-34-1) in which Gordon
Welchman describes in detail his work at Bletchley Park breaking
Enigma ciphers. His is the only book written by someone who
worked at Bletchley throughout the whole war, and it remains a
unique first-hand account of the problems faced, and overcome, by
the mathematicians in the forefront of the attack on Enigma.

Top Secret Ultra (978-0-947712-41-9) has a breadth of coverage,
and an authenticity, which make it an unrivalled one-volume
account of the Enigma machine, the way its ciphers were broken,
the production of 'Ultra' from a sea of decrypts, and the influence
this information had on the conduct of the war. Its author was an
Intelligence Officer, who spent almost all of the war at Bletchley.

**The Colossus Computer, 1943-1996, and how it helped to break
the German Lorenz cipher in WWII (978-0-947712-36-5)**
provides an excellent introduction to the creation of the world's first
programmable computer. This was built (by the Post Office
Research Laboratory) to help the Bletchley Park codebreakers in
their search for the settings of Germany's most sophisticated cipher
machines. In 1996, the author succeeded in building a full-size
working replica of Colossus, now on display at Bletchley.

My Road to Bletchley Park (978-0-947712-44-0), by a WOP/
MSR stationed at Bletchley from 1942 to 1945, gives a lively personal account of the life and work of those dedicated women whose
skills and attention to detail were essential to the efficient functioning of the production line of Intelligence that was Bletchley.

**Harold 'Doc' Keen & the Bletchley Park Bombe (978-0-947712-
42-6)** tells, for the first time, of the work of the man who actually
designed Bletchley's amazing 'bombes', huge devices which
speeded up the search for the settings of the Enigma machines.

*All these can be obtained from the publishers,
whose contact details may be found overleaf.*

. . . *The Codebreakers* . . .

Doctor Mark Baldwin has delivered over two hundred presentations on Second World War codebreaking and related Intelligence topics, with particular reference to the Enigma machine, and the work of Bletchley Park. His presentations are usually followed by a hands-on demonstration of one of the few surviving original Enigma machines, thus providing members of the audience with the chance to operate this iconic device for themselves.

Presentations have been given to professional and technical audiences, to schools, and to the general public, throughout Great Britain, and also in Poland and Germany, and on cruise liners. Dr Baldwin welcomes enquiries from organisations and institutions interested in a presentation on this subject.

Contact details:

c/o M & M Baldwin, 24 High Street,
Cleobury Mortimer, Kidderminster DY14 8BY, England
Tel 01299 270110
email: enigma@mbaldwin.free-online.co.uk